Hamp & Doc

Lynn "Doc" Skinner and the Lionel Hampton Jazz Festival

"To know 'Doc' Skinner, is to love him. How could one not love a man whose infectious enthusiasm has inspired thousands of students, teachers, and audiences alike to expand their knowledge and understanding of jazz?

As the director of the Lionel Hampton Jazz Festival, Doc's passion exuded like a beacon attracting the world's greatest jazz musicians and journalists to share their talent, experience, and support. His vision of ensuring the perpetuation of the art form by exposing young people to the music of the masters through performance and education was ingenious!

As a guest artist at the LHJF 19 times, I witnessed life-changing transformations of thousands of young people through the creative and inspirational effect of jazz. Yes, I'm proud to say I know Lynn 'Doc' Skinner ... and I love him dearly for his magnificent contributions to the world of jazz!" — DEE DANIELS

"The Lionel Hampton Jazz Festival in Moscow, Idaho, has been one of the most important events in the history of jazz for its musicality and amazing scope. Hundreds of significant jazz musicians have appeared there. Thanks to Lynn 'Doc' Skinner, its director, 'chief arranger' and inspiration to the next generation, the festival is still vibrantly in existence." — CLAUDIO RODITI

"Every year I would attend the Festival beginning in 1992 with Ray Brown's trio, Doc Skinner would look me in the eyes at virtually every soundcheck and evening show, to ask me once again with humble and caring concern to hear the full truth of how I was feeling. With all the people surrounding him, he would always take time whenever I was around him at the Festival to express in a language free of clichés or patter, that to him I was a very special human, and to let me know that he cared about my life. When I told him that I was dealing with a minor drug problem, Doc seemed saddened and he showed me such compassion, no judgement, and a gentle but genuine fatherly concern for my life. That's how Doc Skinner treated me as a guest artist of the Festival. If ever I met an angel, it's Doc Skinner." — BENNY GREEN

"Dr. Lynn Skinner has made a very important contribution to jazz education in his positions as director for the Lionel Hampton Jazz Festival and as a member of the faculty of the University of Idaho. His enthusiasm and advocacy for the music were a pleasure to behold. I'm very grateful to have Dr. Skinner as a friend, and I have many wonderful memories of my time with him in Moscow." — JOHN STOWELL

"Dr. Lynn Skinner, the man who changed our destiny, our life ... The musician, composer, pianist, producer, whose talent, energy, and infinite devotion to music, together with the legendary Lionel Hampton, contributed to establishing one of the largest festivals in the USA." — LEONID VINTSKEVICH

Hamp & Doc

Lynn "Doc" Skinner
and the
Lionel Hampton
Jazz Festival

a memoir

Dr. Lynn J. "Doc" Skinner

as told to Alan Jay Solan

INKWATER
PRESS

PORTLAND•OREGON
INKWATERPRESS.COM

Edited by Andrew Durkin
Cover and interior design by Masha Shubin
LHJF photos courtesy of University of Idaho Photo Services

Publisher: Inkwater Press | www.inkwaterpress.com

Paperback ISBN-13 978-1-62901-586-6 | ISBN-10 1-62901-586-5
Hardback ISBN-13 978-1-62901-587-3 | ISBN-10 1-62901-587-3
Kindle   ISBN-13 978-1-62901-606-1 | ISBN-10 1-62901-606-3

1 3 5 7 9 10 8 6 4 2

Dedicated to my wife of fifty-six years,
ELVON SKINNER
(1941–2016)

Losing Elvon was a huge loss in my life. She was my high school sweetheart, and we started dating when she was fourteen. We were married in the Logan Temple in 1960. We both graduated from college together, and both of us had signed a contract to teach in the Madison Schools in Rexburg, Idaho. With our first baby on the way, Elvon decided to be a stay-at-home mother. Elvon spent her life being dedicated to her children and to my thousands of students.

I almost gave up on doing this book because
of the loss of my sweetheart.

Elvon is the mother of three: Tera, Marc, and Matthew.
She is the Grandma to fourteen incredible
grandchildren and seven great-grandchildren.

She always looked for ways to lift those around her through
simple service, kindness, and her warm, beautiful smile.

In her very special way, Elvon was a sister, mother,
or grandma to anyone who came in our home.

Contents

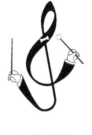

CHAPTER 1

Ladies and Gentlemen ... Lionel Hampton!

PEOPLE USED TO SAY THAT WHEN LIONEL HAMPTON walked onstage and the band started to play, forty years would drop from his body and he would go to work like a young man. That certainly was true when I first met him, on March 3, 1984, when he came to Moscow, Idaho, to perform for the first time at the jazz festival that soon would be renamed in his honor. He turned it all up a notch when he saw so many young people excited to hear him play.

I had been working for a year and a half to get Hamp to come to the festival. I tried to get him for the 1983 festival, but he was scheduled to play a concert in Washington, DC. He came in 1984, the same year as Sarah Vaughan. Hamp performed the night after

Here I am picking up Hamp at his motel in Moscow in 1986.

Sarah, and my first meeting with him took place in his dressing room just before his concert. One of his trombone players, a former student of mine named Chris Gulhaugen, introduced us.

Hamp asked me to introduce him before his performance, and his manager gave me some biographical material to work with. I gave Hamp quite an introduction. He had all these awards and honors: everything from being named American Goodwill Ambassador by President Dwight Eisenhower in 1957, to a Papal Medal from Pope Paul VI, and honorary doctorates from Pepperdine University, the University of Louisiana-Xavier, Howard University, and the State University of New York. He even had a star on the Hollywood Walk of Fame.

Four years later he received an honorary doctorate from the University of Idaho.

The experience of introducing Hamp just blew my mind. Because as I met Hamp on that stage, he put his arms around me and gave me a big hug as if he'd known me all his life. I realized I was standing next to a true jazz legend. I gave him that welcome, he came out on stage, and man, the band played a *show*.

Something Hamp used to do in those days—frequently in Europe and less often in the US—was to have his horn players go out into the audience to play. The rhythm section would stay up on the stage and the horn players would go out and start walking and dancing through the audience. When the students saw that, they got out of their seats and started marching and dancing right behind them.

Hamp's musicians just thought this was incredible, and they played it to the hilt. When they came back up on stage, Hamp told the young people in the audience it was one of his greatest moments to be there with them. Hundreds of kids stood and started yelling and cheering for him. He said he'd played all over the world, but in the United States, he rarely saw an audience get up and follow the band around and dance in the aisles like he had seen that night. Ray Brown later told me he had seen that happen when he was in high school and saw Hamp's big band perform in Pittsburgh.

Lionel Hampton was the perfect person—along with his friends, the greatest jazz musicians in the world—to touch the lives of the students who came to the festival. He just had a way of doing things that brought excitement to the audience. He would raise his vibe mallets in the air and the audience would jump up and start screaming. He just brought this out in people. And as for his music, there's no doubt he was one of the greatest players of all time.

After the concert, we had a gathering for Hamp and his band. There were several kinds of food there, but when Hamp found out we had spaghetti and meatballs, he got excited. Hamp loved spaghetti and meatballs. Another of his favorite dishes was fresh trout and mashed Idaho potatoes with chicken gravy.

Later, after Hamp started coming to the festival every year, people in the community would invite him to their homes for dinner. A woman named Vera White, who was a writer for the local newspaper and an excellent cook, loved to have Hamp come to her place during the festival. Her brother, who was a Catholic priest in Spokane, Washington, was also a great cook, and he would come down to Moscow, and they would make special meals for Hamp. Sometimes they'd get him so full of food it was hard for him to get up on stage and perform. We had to get a couple cups of black coffee in him to get him going.

When Hamp found out I was at the post-concert gathering after his first show, he asked to see me. He wanted to know more about what was happening to bring all of these kids together in one place to hear a jazz concert. He said, "I'm impressed. What are you doing?"

I explained my personal passion and mission for the festival, which was to provide an experience in jazz for young people—one unlike any other in the world. I wanted to create a place where the world's greatest jazz artists would come, not only to perform, but also to do workshops and clinics to inspire the young people who would be tomorrow's leaders.

Hamp loved this vision. In fact, he was so pleased to hear my philosophy of what a jazz festival should do for young people that he pulled out his checkbook and wrote a $15,000 check to help ensure the future of the festival. He said, "Take this and start a little endowment fund for the festival. Gradually, people will add to that as the years go by."

Then we exchanged business cards, and he gave me his home phone number. He said, "Call me anytime, Doc. If you need help with artists, let me know. A heck of a lot of guys played in my band at one time or another."

CHAPTER 2

Fanning the
Flame of Jazz

IN 1971, AFTER TEACHING IN THE IDAHO PUBLIC
schools for nine years and earning my master's in music performance and doctorate in music education along the way, I was
hired by the University of Idaho in Moscow. I never imagined
that in a matter of a few years I would become the director of
a jazz festival that would be known around the world, and that
I would become great friends with its namesake, the legendary
Lionel Hampton.

The event that became the Lionel Hampton Jazz Festival was
then called the University of Idaho Jazz Festival. It was started
in 1968 by a brilliant music education professor and jazz lover
named Bruce Bray, who was my predecessor in music education
at UI. It was created as a venue for high school musicians to play
and be adjudicated. The first year of the festival, there were

Here I am in 1972, in my first year as a professor at the University of Idaho.

twelve entries. The following year, David Seiler and Bob Spevacek took over running the event.

My friend, Rich Werner, a professor of trumpet, had been hired at UI the same year as me. One of his duties was to direct the jazz festival, and he asked if I'd help him out. I had run high school band and vocal competitions for nine years; I could do scheduling and those kinds of things with my eyes closed. Rich was a very bright guy, but he hadn't done a whole lot of those things. So, in 1972, I started helping him with scheduling. I think that first year I may even have judged some groups to help out. I did that three or four years in a row. I moved equipment, greeted people, and met the bus drivers and the teachers who brought the students. I welcomed them to the campus and made sure everything was going well and that the judges were taken care of. I was there to help my friend, because I knew running the festival was a big job. Little did I know how big the job really was.

When I started helping with the festival, it had grown from a dozen high school groups to about fifty. As a music professor, one of my assignments was to work with the student chapter of what was then called the Music Educators National Conference, so

I encouraged the students in the chapter to help with the festival. Soon those students and I were helping Rich in any way we could. That included moving risers, chairs, and music stands, and helping set up the sound system at the university's Student Union Building.

At that time, the festival took place the first Friday and Saturday of March. Besides a few people in the school of music who were helping with it, there weren't many people on campus who even realized the festival was happening. No one was taking any official photographs, so there aren't any photos of the groups that performed in those early years. There just wasn't really that much interest in the festival at that time.

In the fall of 1976, Rich took a job at the University of Wyoming, and Bill Billingsley, the director of the school of music, asked if I would take over the jazz festival for the coming year. With Rich gone, there was no one else to run it. I agreed to take it over for a year—and that year turned into thirty-one years. The first year I took over was a great experience for me, and it never stopped being great. I never once went to work without being excited about helping young people experience jazz.

As soon as I took over the festival, I started thinking about how to best help the students who attended. There is no way you can touch the soul of a human being with music that's done poorly. We might think we were doing something, but it wasn't going to truly reach them until it was done right. That has been my motto about music my whole life: "If it's not done right, let's not do it at all." I knew if we didn't do it with jazz, if we didn't do it with classical music, we were not going to reach young student musicians.

By the early 1980s the festival was starting to get a little better known, but when we brought in Hamp and renamed the festival in 1985, that changed everything. It seemed like every major jazz magazine, as well as magazines and newspapers from around the world, wrote about the naming of the Lionel Hampton Jazz Festival. Not only was it the first student-oriented festival of its kind, it was named for a jazz musician, and an African American. When artists found out about it, my phone started ringing off the hook. For years afterward, I got calls from people who had played with Hamp and wanted to be a part of that whole scene again. But that was Hamp. He knew so many people, and he was so good with people. I think naming the festival after Hamp, and the media coverage that followed, gave him the tribute and the honor he deserved.

Never Wish
for the End
of a Phrase

THE MEDIA BARRAGE THAT CAME IN 1985, WITH THE renaming of the festival, and again in 1987, when the university's music school was renamed the Lionel Hampton School of Music, was not the first time the national media had taken an interest in Moscow's jazz festival.

When Ella Fitzgerald came to the festival in 1982, there were lots of newspaper stories about it, and that really helped publicize the festival. Having a name like Ella Fitzgerald just blew everybody away. The number of students who came that year was amazing. As I recall, there were about five thousand.

As I began working to get Ella Fitzgerald to the festival, school officials told me the university simply could not afford to cover her $20,000 fee by itself and that, without some outside financial support, the university would not be able to bring her in.

I was in southern Idaho in October for my wife's parents' fiftieth wedding anniversary, and I told my oldest sister the university wouldn't be able to bring Ella to the festival without some financial help. She told me Chevron was drilling in the area and suggested the company might like do something to counteract the image it was getting from the rough-looking characters it had working on its oil rigs. I went to where Chevron was drilling and asked to talk to the head man. I asked him if it would be easier for them if Chevron was known for something besides drilling for oil. He said, "Would it ever!" I told him I'd like to get Chevron to support the Ella Fitzgerald concert, and he gave me the name of a person in Denver to call.

The Chevron executive in Denver was excited about the idea, but he said he couldn't make those kinds of decisions. He told me to call a man in the company's Seattle office. As luck would have it, that man was a real jazz fan. When I asked him if Chevron would underwrite an Ella Fitzgerald concert, he thought it was a great idea, but he said that the decision would have to come from Chevron headquarters in San Francisco.

"The good news," he said, "is one of the vice presidents for Chevron is a graduate of the University of Idaho." He told me the people who could make the decision were on their way to Dallas, but that he would contact them as soon as possible. About three hours later, he called me and said, "This must have been good, Doc. They called me immediately when they hit the ground in Dallas and said, 'We're on.'"

So Chevron became an underwriter for the concert. It was a dream come true. One of the greatest jazz singers of all time was coming to the University of Idaho's jazz festival. The minute I had the support from Chevron, I was able to get permission to bring her here, because $20,000 was really quite a lot of money in those days, and I don't think the University of Idaho had ever done anything like that before.

Ella would perform on Saturday night and George Shearing, one of the world's greatest jazz pianists, would perform on Friday night. Ticket prices for Ella's concert ranged from six dollars and fifty cents to twelve dollars. Even though I still had to move the chairs in Memorial Gym after the concert, it was the treat of a lifetime to have Ella Fitzgerald and George Shearing at the festival.

Before Ella's performance, I would say there were fewer than half a dozen upper administrators on campus who were even aware that the school had a jazz festival. I had been asked to serve on a committee to look at something for the provost, and we were sitting in a meeting when somebody said, "Hey, Doc, who's coming to the festival this year?"

I thought the provost's jaw would hit the table when I said, "Well, I just got some support from Chevron. We're bringing in Ella Fitzgerald."

After the meeting, the provost and I walked over to his office, and I told him what was going on with the festival, how it was on its way up. He just kept saying, "I had no idea, I had no idea." He told me he'd talk to Joe Geiger, the university's financial vice president, to see about getting the festival more support from the university. After that, it was amazing how things changed in terms of the support. There still wasn't enough of a budget to do any major advertising, but there were so many articles written about Ella's visit that they provided all the advertising we needed.

A couple of days before Ella's concert, I got a call from Joe Geiger. He said, "Doc, I've just been over to Memorial Gym, and I'm sick to my stomach." I said, "What's the matter, Joe?" He said, "Have you noticed how terrible the stage curtain is?" I agreed the old curtain was indeed terrible. He asked me to meet him at the gym in fifteen minutes. When I got there, he said, "Let's replace this with a beautiful black curtain, so that when Ella gets onstage she'll feel like she's on a very special stage that was made just for her." That really got me. Here was someone in the upper administration who was trying to look out for the festival.

I lost track of the number of phone calls I got from newspaper people all over the world before Ella's concert. Often they called to check out rumors.

"We heard Ella Fitzgerald isn't coming. Is that true?"

Then, a few days later, more calls: "We've heard again that Ella Fitzgerald isn't coming."

I had no idea where the rumors were coming from, but none of them were true. Ella was coming to the festival. We had brochures and posters with her photograph that we sent to the schools that participated in the jazz festival. She had been in a television commercial for Memorex cassette tapes, where she sang a note and a glass broke. Everyone had seen the commercial, and all the students knew who Ella Fitzgerald was. I believe it made them feel her visit was an important event and that they should be there.

We didn't know at the time that Ella's nephew had recently been killed in an accident, and that she was so upset that she almost decided it would be too much for her to perform. But a woman named Mary Jane Outwater, who worked with Norman Granz, told me Ella wanted and needed to be at the festival. She was such an incredible lady. She didn't finish performing until after midnight.

The year Ella came to the festival, with pianist Jimmy Rowles, it was still taking place in Memorial Gym. In those days, the only official help I had with the festival was a single graduate student. I got started about four thirty every morning. In fact, my son, Marc, and one of his friends used to get up in the morning with me and come over and start moving risers and chairs so that we'd have them in place to start the day's events. There was nothing like the organized volunteer system the festival has today. I remember there were something like 1,100 chairs on the campus and we needed around 2,500 more. We went to Washington State University, across the border in Pullman. We went everywhere we could to get chairs to fill up Memorial Gym for Ella's concert.

The University of Idaho men's basketball team was across campus in the Kibbie Dome, playing for the Big Sky Championship on the same night, and Ella didn't want to start her concert until the game had ended. She eventually decided to start, but she told me to let her know when the game was over, and who won—especially, she said, if it was "our Vandals." She said she'd scat the outcome of the game into one of her songs. When the Vandals won, I gave her a smile and a thumbs-up, and sure enough, she scatted into the song she was singing that the Vandals had won the game. The crowd went nuts, because the way she did it was so classy. I sat there thinking: How could this be? This is probably the greatest vocalist in the world, in my opinion, and here she was.

After the concert, I asked Ella if she'd be willing to go to the home of Dean Vetruss, the manager of the Student Union Building, to meet the mayor and some other people. Ella said, "As long as you're there with me, Doc, I'll be fine."

I remember she had this beautiful, full-length black mink coat, and Dean said, "Ma'am, I'd be happy to take your coat." Ella said, "I'll bet you would!" She was just teasing him, of course, but she said, "I'll just keep it here with me."

Besides the mayor, we had people out of Boise and from throughout the region who wanted to meet Ella. Professors and staff, the university president, deans and vice presidents lined up, and Ella sat there for nearly two hours and greeted people. When it was all over she said, "Now, Doc, I want just a moment with you." I told her I was heavily involved in music education and did clinics and workshops all over the United States and Canada all year long. We sat and talked for a while, and she was so gracious. She said, "It's so important, what you're doing."

She went on, "Is there something you'd like to ask me? You could use an Ella Fitzgerald quote!" So, of course, I said, "You know, that would be great, something that would work for kids who are doing music. It doesn't matter what it is they are doing. Music is music. What would be a great quote?"

And she said, "Never wish for the end of a phrase."

I have used that with choirs, bands, orchestras, solo kids, you name it, and they just say, "Oh, wow!" because they know that very often the phrase gets cut off a little short in some way. We don't really get to the very last moment. The richest moment is the very ending of the note, and usually it gets cut off too soon.

Ella's visit brought a lot of press and drew people to the festival. People called from all over, saying, "How do we get there? How do we do this? I'd like to come from so-and-so." New schools started taking part in the festival. In terms of touching the lives of young people, Ella's performance was the greatest ever, because most of us who heard her that night would never have the opportunity to hear her again. After her performance, I started getting letters from students who had attended her concert. One of them was from a young man who said he'd been having various personal struggles. "Then I came to the concert, and I heard Ella sing, and all those feelings went away," he said. "I became a whole person because of Ella."

Later, a young man from Boise, Idaho, came to the festival. He played two or three tunes with Hamp's band, plus his own stuff. He even played one of Hamp's tunes for Hamp. When the concert was over, he told me he had attended Ella's 1982 festival concert when he was in the high school choir. He said hearing Ella sing that night, watching how the audience responded to her, and how she had the ability to touch the soul of every person there, literally changed his life.

He said, "I made a decision that night, that if the man upstairs wanted me to do this, he would help me find a way." Not long after that, he hooked up with the great pianist Gene Harris, who also lived in Boise. Gene became one of his teachers and helped him on the way. That young man's name was Curtis Stigers, and now he's performing all over the world.

A few years later, in 1993, Chevron was going through some major corporate problems. Gas prices were not good, and the company was in financial trouble. The board of directors decided the company would no longer support the festival financially. I appreciated the support the company had given the festival over the years. All we could do was move on and find other ways to keep it going. I'm sure that was a tough time for Chevron, but it wasn't a tough time for the jazz festival. It just kept growing. In the 1990s, there were more entries every year. By 1996, the number of entries had grown from fifty—when I took over the festival—to 575.

All the artists gave everything they had. The festival always started on a Wednesday, and they'd come backstage after the first concert and say, "I never thought I'd see anything like that." Then Thursday night it would climb another level, and then Friday night another, until Saturday, when they'd say, "I can't believe this!"

CHAPTER 4

The Original "Lionel Hampton School"

IT SEEMS PERFECTLY LOGICAL TO ME THAT LIONEL Hampton should have a jazz festival and a music school named after him. After all, from the very beginning of his long career as a musician and bandleader, Hamp always sought to nurture and develop the talents of others. He was a true teacher in every sense of the word.

Hamp was born in Louisville, Kentucky, in 1908. He lived in Alabama and then in Chicago. That's where he lived when he started playing drums at a Catholic school and as a member of the *Chicago Defender* Newsboys' Band.

He started playing professionally in 1927, as a drummer in Les Hite's band. Hamp's connection with the vibraphone is said to have begun in 1930, at a recording session in Los Angeles with

Louis Armstrong. When Louis heard Hamp play, they decided to record some tunes featuring Hamp on the vibes. They recorded "Memories of You" later that year and "Shine" in 1931.

In 1936, Hamp joined Benny Goodman's trio, which included Teddy Wilson on piano and Gene Krupa on drums. The Benny Goodman Quartet performed at Carnegie Hall in 1938, and recorded several tunes that featured Hamp on vibes, one of the best-known being "Stompin' at the Savoy."

Hamp was with Benny Goodman until 1940, when he left to start his own big band, which he led for the rest of his life, and where the real "Lionel Hampton School of Music" began. Being in the Lionel Hampton Big Band really was like attending a prestigious, high-caliber school for jazz. It was the real deal, and when you earned your "diploma" from Hamp, it meant something, and it opened a lot of doors. Many, many of the musicians who played in Hamp's band went on to become jazz legends in their own right: Dexter Gordon, Fats Navarro, Arnett Cobb, Benny Golson, Quincy Jones, Dinah Washington, Aretha Franklin, and Illinois Jacquet, to name a few.

It's rare to see a photo of Hamp without a huge smile on his face. He smiled not only when he was performing, but also when he was talking about music or listening to someone play. He had that same unbounded joy I have felt about music since I was a little boy.

But you couldn't let that big smile fool you. Yes, Hamp loved to laugh and have fun, but he was first of all a musician and bandleader. Sometimes a person might only play in his band for six weeks, but no matter how briefly they played in Hamp's band, they never forgot what it was like to rehearse with him, because Hamp wanted things done right.

Hamp was ninety years old at the 1999 festival, and his health wasn't great. I remember him sitting in a chair with his head down during a rehearsal, while I took notes and did some other things he'd asked me to do. I thought maybe he was asleep—but all of a sudden he stood up and stopped the band and said, "Third trumpet player, if you ever miss that note again, you're going home."

I'll tell you, there were no other wrong notes played.

CHAPTER 5

A House of
Music and Love

LIONEL HAMPTON WAS AN INCREDIBLE MAN, AND HIS belief in me and in the Lionel Hampton Jazz Festival has been one of the most positive and uplifting experiences of my life. Because of Lionel Hampton, I've had the opportunity to meet and work with some of the world's greatest jazz artists. Because of Lionel Hampton, the lives of thousands of young people have been positively affected. Because of Lionel Hampton, the great American art form of jazz continues to be passed on to new generations. And because of Lionel Hampton, I have a story I want to tell.

This story is about my relationship with Lionel Hampton and my experiences as director of the Lionel Hampton Jazz Festival, but it's about much more than that. The story doesn't begin in 1984, when I first met Lionel Hampton. It doesn't begin in 1977, when I took over direction of the festival, or in 1971, when I first

This is the ranch where I grew up. I returned there in 1973, after my dad died, and built this wagon wheel fence.

came to the University of Idaho. The story of my lifelong love of music begins with my parents.

I was born on November 20, 1940, in the small southern Idaho community of Nounan (population eighty). I was the fourth child of Lester and Lola Mary Skinner. My great-grandfather had settled that part of the country at the request of Brigham Young, and nearby Skinner Canyon and Skinner Creek are named for our family.

I grew up with two older sisters, an older brother, and a younger sister. Growing up, my siblings and I were very close, and we rarely had a cross word or any kind of a fight with each other—although there was the time when I was about five and my brother convinced me to pee on an electric fence. I used to

19

tell people the only thing more painful than that was listening to a band that was out of tune.

When I was four, my dad bought another ranch, and we moved to a house that was directly across the street from the community's two-room schoolhouse. I completed my first six grades in that school; there were three or four kids in each grade. There was no music program, but there was an old piano on the stage, and often during recess I'd go up and play it. All the kids would gather around and start singing, and that was the school's music program.

Ours was a very musical home, and we always had a piano.

Here I am visiting home in Nounan, Idaho, after my dad died.

When we moved to our new house, which actually was a very old house that had been fixed up, my father bought my mother a Hammond organ—the kind with the big speakers, like the ones used in churches. This was around 1945, so it was a tough time to get things like that. Then he bought her a Lester piano, and a little later a Mason & Hamlin, which was a very good piano.

My mother was a very beautiful and distinguished blonde, and I remember how proud my father was of her. She had her hair done at the beauty parlor once a week, and she always took great pride in how she looked. My dad wasn't a musician, but he loved to hear my mom play. Sometimes he'd make her laugh by playing simple little made-up songs on the piano. He'd sit down with a flourish and say, "Here's a little concert for you."

My mother was kind, gentle, loving, talented, and fun. She had a great sense of humor, a very dry wit, and she loved the English language. She was the valedictorian of her high school class and took great pride in writing properly. If I showed her something I had written, she wanted it to be done the way it should be, with correct grammar.

My mom had grown up playing dance tunes, and had even played in a dance orchestra when she was a young girl. She knew hundreds of tunes—any kind of tune you would dance to. My mother's family couldn't afford music lessons, so she taught herself how to read music. One day someone at school showed her the major scale, and she figured out how to play it in every key, all the rhythms, everything. So, when I was very young, she started playing for me.

I remember her playing "I Love You Truly," and lots of waltzes—particularly "The Missouri Waltz" and "The Tennessee Waltz." People in the 1940s used to love to dance to those old tunes. My mother played for dance nights at church, so she knew all these tunes off the top of her head. She taught me to play those tunes—or rather just the basic chords, because once I heard the tune, I could play the melody.

So I started playing the piano even before I started taking lessons. I was four years old, and I could already play tunes by ear. That was really the start of my love of music. People would come to our house and my mom would play while they sang, and if they didn't sing in tune, she'd try to help them a little bit. I listened to all that, and developed an incredible sense of how to play in tune.

My mother told me I started to talk at an early age, but the most amazing thing to her was that I could sing melodies even before I could talk. My mother played musical games with me to

This is me around age four, when I started taking piano lessons.

see if I could recognize notes she played on the piano. I could do it most of the time, but I'd get us off track when I started making my own melodies out of the notes she had played.

I started piano lessons when I was four. (I tell people I rode my tricycle uphill both ways on a gravel road.) I discovered the teacher only needed to play the piece once for me to learn it. I distinctly remember one of the first pieces I learned was by Robert Schumann. In fact, I played it for my first recital. It was a little watered-down version, but it was actually very difficult. We started on some pretty advanced stuff.

The thing was, if I could get the teacher to play a tune for me—any tune—I'd go home and practice it and have it perfect the next week. But if I would have had to sight-read it, I'd have been in deep trouble. Actually, the teacher and my mom both thought I was reading it at the time, but I later took lessons from another teacher, and she not only confirmed that I couldn't read music but also that I needed glasses.

I was in church one day when I was maybe nine or ten years old, and my mother was playing the organ. As she played the hymns, all of a sudden I realized I could hear the parts of the songs. A ladies' trio used to practice at our home, so I had heard harmonizing and so forth, and I thought it was neat that they could just look at the music and know what it sounded like. I distinctly remember that day in church. We were singing the sacrament hymn. I was listening carefully, and all of a sudden I looked at the tenor notes and the bass notes in the hymnal, and I could hear them before they were played.

Years later that made an incredible difference when I was playing trombone with a big band at a large hotel in Ogden, Utah. The other members of the band were amazed at how well I could read music. I told them I just looked at the music and I could hear it.

That all started with that one experience that day in church.

I didn't always wear a suit and tie. Here I am as a high school senior. I played basketball every year of high school at Montpelier High.

CHAPTER 6

Life Lessons
from My Dad

MY DAD RAISED SHEEP, AMONG OTHER ANIMALS, AND we had a herd of about 1,500. Every once in a while a ewe cannot or will not raise her lamb. Those lambs are called "bum lambs," and one year when I was about seven, my father gave me a bum lamb that I named Billy. I taught Billy to suck from a bottle with a nipple on it, and later how to drink from a pan made from the lid of an old ten-gallon milk can. My father said he had never seen this done with a sheep.

Billy was incredible. I could call him and even when he was with other sheep, he would come to me. However, my gender evaluation was mistaken, because when Billy became old enough, *she* had twins. Billy brought her lambs to see me, and they drank from the same milk can lid she used to use.

I was in the house having lunch one day, when the neighbor passed through our place with his entire herd of seven or eight bands of sheep—as many as 9,000 animals. My father raised his eyebrow and said, "Joe"—he always called me by my middle name—"where is Billy?" I went outside and realized she must have gone with the neighbor's herd. I was sure she was lost forever. My dad tried to console me and told me we would see how good of a master I was. We hooked a trailer to the car and went to find Billy.

When we arrived at the place where the sheep were gathered before being let loose to graze, I couldn't imagine how we would ever find Billy. I had never seen so many sheep in one place in my life. My dad knew better, though, and he lifted me up onto the fence and told me to call Billy with all my might. I began calling her name, and after what seemed like an eternity to me, my dad saw some movement in the middle of that enormous flock. It took about half an hour for Billy to make her way to my side with her twins.

My dad lifted Billy and her twins over the fence and placed them in our little trailer. Then he told me what a good master I was, because I knew "the one" was so important. I had searched and brought the lost one back to the fold. He was referring to the parable of Jesus, told in Matthew and Luke, about the shepherd who left his ninety-nine sheep to search for the one that was lost. My dad always had a way of tying things back to the scriptures.

My dad was always telling me stories when I worked with him on the ranch as a boy. And he wasn't above a joke now and then either. Once, when we were cleaning out an enormous chicken coop, he came over to me and said, "Well, that was just awful!"

"What's the matter, Dad?"

"I dropped my chewing gum."

"Oh, that's too bad."

"Yeah, it really is. It took me three tries to find it!"

Dad could always make us laugh, but many of his stories were meant to teach us about life.

He told me a story about something that happened to him when he was around twelve years old. He and a friend wanted to take their horses across a train trestle over the Bear River. His father told him not to do it, but he sneaked away one Sunday and did it anyway.

Apparently, it was quite exciting to go across the trestle on a horse, looking down through the railroad ties at the river below. But it also was very dangerous. After he and his friend had crossed the trestle a few times, my dad suggested they do it once more before heading home. They were almost across when my dad's horse slipped and all four legs went between the ties. My dad was wondering what to do when he heard a train whistle and knew a train was less than a mile away. All he had time to do was remove the horse's saddle and bridle and get down from the trestle himself. A few moments later the train came around the bend, traveling too fast to stop, and ran over the horse. You can imagine how horrible it was to see such a thing.

My dad had to walk five miles back home, carrying his horse's saddle, saddle blanket, and bridle. When his father saw him coming, he knew what had happened. He'd been afraid it would happen someday, and he'd warned my father and his friends about the danger. But instead of being angry or punishing him, all he said was, "If only you would have listened."

One winter when I was about six or seven years old, it had been snowing really hard. The snow was six feet deep in some places. But the livestock had to be fed, and I asked my dad if I could go with him on the sleigh when he brought a load of hay to the cows.

We hooked the sleigh to our horses, Glen and Turk, loaded up with hay, and headed out into the storm toward the pasture. It was quite cold, especially for a little kid, but my dad tried to take our minds off the cold by telling me stories. We were both laughing away, when all of a sudden the sleigh came to a dead stop. The horses had tried to go through a snowdrift, but it was too deep and the runners of the sleigh had caught. We were stuck.

My dad said that if he could just get the horses to give one good, strong pull it would pop the sleigh loose from the snowdrift. Glen was the smaller horse, weighing about 1,200 pounds, while

Turk probably weighed 2,000 pounds. When my dad gave the command, Glen pulled with all his might, while Turk definitely took a more leisurely approach. In fact, Glen pulled so hard he literally flipped over onto his back and came loose from his harness.

My dad got Glen up again and re-hooked the harness, then walked over to Turk. I never knew what my dad said, but he must have gotten through to him, because when we got back in the sleigh and my dad gave the command again, both horses pulled and the sleigh popped out of the snowdrift. We got to the field, put the hay in the rack, and headed back home. This time we were going almost full speed when we hit that snowdrift, and we just busted right through it like a bulldozer.

That day I learned something important about pulling together and working as a team, and it has stayed with me my whole life. For one thing, I don't think Turk could have pulled that sleigh loose by himself—even though he was much larger and stronger than Glen. They had to work together to free the sleigh.

Throughout my career I knew that if I had someone on my team and they worked hard and worked with me, we could get an awful lot done. It happened with my staff in the jazz festival office. I wanted every one of them to feel important. But they had a job to do, and I wanted them to do it. I wanted everyone to be pulling as hard as everybody else. It was amazing, the things we were able to accomplish with that attitude. I always felt my dad was on my "team" as well. The most wonderful thing about my dad was his support. No matter what I was doing, he was there to support and encourage me.

If I had to name the most important thing I learned from my dad, it would be work ethic. He told me, "There will never be an eight-to-five gig. They don't exist." Some people work from eight to five, but when they leave, there is still more work to be done. On a ranch, that could mean feeding or caring for the livestock, or whatever needed to be done to keep the operation going. But no matter what your job was, the key was appreciating the value of good, hard work.

Another important thing he taught me is that if you love what you're doing, no matter what it is, the work doesn't seem as heavy. I think that was why I was willing to work so hard in my career, right from the start. I didn't keep working on the ranch with my father and brother, but I took the work ethic I learned from them with me to the Rexburg-Madison School District, the University of Idaho, and the Lionel Hampton Jazz Festival.

My dad had a serious heart attack during the first year I was working at the University of Idaho, and he died the following year. I remember going to see him in his hospital room, knowing that he was not going to make it. I was fortunate enough to help give him a blessing of being able to speak to all of his children for the last time. As everyone was leaving the room, he asked me to stay. I came back and put my arms around him, and he said, "I wanted you to know you made the right decision when you went to the University of Idaho. That's where you were supposed to be. I felt that, but I didn't want to tell you until you'd made the decision. I just wanted you to know how proud I am of you."

I'm sure my dad now knows of my experiences with the Lionel Hampton Jazz Festival.

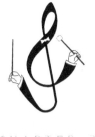

CHAPTER 7

A Horn Blows in Idaho

AFTER I FINISHED SIXTH GRADE, MY SCHOOL STOPPED offering seventh and eighth grade, so I went to junior high about fifteen miles away in Montpelier, Idaho. Montpelier had about three thousand people and was considered the "big town" in the area. My oldest sister was working for a dentist there, so I already knew a couple of kids in town. I was eleven years old and already nearly five foot eleven. There was no one that tall in the seventh grade—and I was young for a seventh grader, too, because I started school when I was five.

I had lots of friends, and many of them wanted me to play basketball with them. I loved to do that, but what I really wanted was to play in the school band. Many of my friends were in the band, and I'd been looking forward to junior high and seeing if I could get in it too. One day I asked a girl who sat next to me if she knew anything about getting into the band, and she said, "Well, my dad's the band director. I'll check with him and see." Her name was Doris Baker, and her father was Wes Baker. Mr. Baker said I'd have to start out with the fourth graders, but that was fine with me. I wanted to play in the band, and I would do whatever it took.

A few days later, my dad went with me to the school when a man was showing all these instruments—trombones, trumpets, drums, clarinets, flutes, saxophones, and other horns. I already knew what I wanted to play. I had already talked about it with my dad, and my dad got right to the point.

"What's the best tenor saxophone you have?"

"A King Super 20 with a solid silver neck and pearl-inlayed keys."

"How much would a horn like that cost?"

"Four hundred dollars."

That was a lot of money. My dad said the same thing he said when he was buying a car or just about anything else: "How much would that be ... *cash?*"

The salesman knocked fifty dollars off the price, and we arranged for the horn to be kept with the band director, where it would be mine for the taking when we came up with the money to pay for it.

When I got home from school the next day, my dad told me to go down to the field and get our best milk cow and bring her up to the barn. I didn't realize then what was happening—I just did as I was told.

Here I am at age eleven in front of Montpelier Junior High School with the saxophone my father sold his best cow to buy for me. I've played that same sax all these years.

After I brought her to the barn, my dad told me a man who had been trying to buy the cow for a long time would be along shortly. He said if he gave us enough money, it would pay for my saxophone.

This man had been to our milking barn several times trying to buy the cow because she was extremely productive—sometimes giving as much as six gallons of milk at a time. But my dad felt so strongly about helping me with what he knew was my dream. I'd always said, even as a young boy, that I wanted to direct music and create music to make people happy. Even as a little boy, I remember feeling in my soul that there was something special about music. My dad realized that. In fact, he'd often send me in from chores early so I could practice the piano.

When the man arrived, my dad immediately asked him, "How much are you willing to pay for this cow?"

"Three twenty-five," he answered.

My dad turned to me and said, "Hey, kid—take the cow back to the field."

Then the man started singing a different tune, as they say.

"No! No! How much do you have to have?"

"It's got to be three fifty," my dad told him, "because that's going to buy this boy a saxophone."

The man just shook his head a little, wrote out a check, loaded up our very best milk cow, and drove away.

I had seen the saxophone in the case, but I hadn't touched it. After my father gave me a check to give to the band director the next day, I was so overcome with emotion that I had to go down to the basement for a minute or two by myself. I shed a few tears because I could hardly believe this had happened to me. And this was not just any saxophone; it was one of the finest saxophones ever made.

It meant so much to me that my dad cared that much—that he would sell his best cow to buy that saxophone. I lay awake most of the night, hearing saxophone players in my head and thinking, "Oh, man, I wonder if I'll ever be able to play something like that!"

The next day I rode home on the bus, holding my saxophone case tightly in my arms. I would have liked to open up the case and look at it, but I didn't want to take it out and then have someone bump it or dink around with it. I wanted to get that saxophone home safely and open it in front of my mom and dad.

My mom had dinner ready when I got home from school. I had chores to do, but my dad said, "Don't worry about your chores tonight. We'll take care of them. You've got that new horn."

I didn't know how to play my new sax, but the band director had given me a book. I figured out how to put on the reed and I put the horn up to my lips and blew. I immediately saw I could get a sound. I looked at the book. It says you play a G like this. I studied the book a little more. G-A-B-C-D. I figured it out. I was playing scales, and it was amazing. It was like my saxophone had figured out how to play itself.

My mom said, "It sounds like you're doing real well. Why don't you bring your saxophone into the living room, and I'll play the piano. We'll play some hymns."

Nobody had told me that you had to transpose, but the minute I walked in, my mom said, "Play a note." So I played a note, and she said, "OK, when you play C, it sounds like B-flat on the piano, so you're going to have to transpose it." I knew what that meant, so I transposed all these hymns to the right key for the saxophone—up one full step—and played dozens of hymns with my mother that night.

I got to the band room early the next afternoon. I strapped on my saxophone and started playing a bunch of scales and hymns. When the band director came in and heard me playing, he said, "What are you doing?"

I said, "Well, I'm just playing my horn."

"Okay," he said. "You're in the junior high band."

So I spent one day in the fourth-grade band, and the next day I was in the junior high band—and the rest is history. I still have that King Super 20. It's the horn I still play today.

CHAPTER 8

A Band of My Own

WHEN I WAS A SOPHOMORE IN HIGH SCHOOL IN 1955, I started a dance band with a few of my friends. We soon figured out we needed a new place to practice, because the high school had very limited hours. I told my mom about it and she said, "Why don't you use our house? Our living room's big enough for a drum set and the music stands." So that's what we did.

I remember our first gig was the junior prom at the high school. It was a little scary because I wasn't sure we had enough tunes. But we did, and we made it through the night. We spent all the money we made buying more sheet music so we could learn more tunes and get more jobs for our little band. Before long, we had a regular Saturday night gig at Bear Lake. The place would be filled with kids from all over the area. Some of them were a little rowdy, but it was still a big kick for me.

Then I heard about a place called Lakota, which was about twenty miles from our regular Saturday night gig. It was also on

Here's a rare shot of the jazz band I started as a sophomore in high school
in 1955. At the left of the photo is Floyd Bunderson, I'm in the center, on
the right is Ronald Jensen, and Glade Tueller is in the back, center.

Bear Lake, but on the Utah side. I went over and talked to the
manager and said, "What if we do a late show? I'll announce it at
our other show, and people can come here at eleven o'clock, and
we'll play until two." He said, "Fine! Welcome to Utah!" I split
the house with him, and sometimes that worked out really well
for both of us.

The first time I played in a large jazz band was at the Utah
State University summer music camp in 1958, right before I
started college there. I played second tenor. They just believed
in me because I could read music so easily. For the rest of his
life, Earl Erickson, the man who ran the camp, had great faith in
everything I tried to do.

I started to buy jazz albums in high school. There was a fur-
niture store in Montpelier that had some records, and I found
some pretty good swing records there. When I went off to college

at Utah State University I discovered that lots of other students were also interested in jazz, so I started buying even more records. I bought records by Lionel Hampton, Ray Brown, Dizzy Gillespie, Stan Getz, Gerry Mulligan, Ella Fitzgerald, and many others. I had a nice collection of records as a very young kid, and I listened to them all the time.

When I started college at Utah State, I found out a radio station out of Salt Lake City—KSL-FM—had a jazz show every night at midnight. We'd be studying and two or three of us would take turns and go out to a car and listen.

My mom and dad always had a record player in the house. When I was a boy, they had lots of 78 rpm records. Many of them were swing bands, and there were also lots of famous singers that my mom loved to listen to. You could put a stack of records on the player, but each record only had one song per side. I got married when I was still in college, and one of the first things my wife Elvon and I bought was a stereo. (More about Elvon shortly.)

I came home from college one weekend and saw that my mom and dad had bought a new hi-fi stereo. My mom also had bought me eight or ten new jazz records—big bands, all kinds of stuff—to take back to school. It meant a lot to me that she realized music was an important thing in my life, and that I wasn't going to give it up.

During my first year of college, I went to hear the Stan Kenton Band, which featured the trumpet players Pete and Conte Candoli. I later found out they were good friends of Lionel Hampton— and we became friends too, after they performed at the festival in Moscow. I also saw George Shearing, Louis Armstrong, and many other great bands and artists who came to Utah State. It was incredible to hear all these great people, and then to have some of them be a part of the Lionel Hampton Jazz Festival years later.

I'll never forget George Shearing. He came to campus in the spring of 1960, and performed in a huge old field house. There was a grand piano in the middle and seating all around. The stage revolved slowly so everybody could eventually see him. I was up close, so I could really see him. He walked up to the piano, sat down, and started to play. After he played the first number he said, "We have a problem here. We have a problem here." And it was just hushed silence. Then he said, "Would somebody please turn on the lights?" The audience was taken aback for a couple seconds, wondering why a blind man wanted to have the lights turned on. Then the crowd exploded in laughter. Shearing smiled and said, "That's what I wanted."

CHAPTER 9

My Mentor Max

I EARNED ALL THREE OF MY DEGREES AT UTAH STATE University in Logan. Logan was fairly close to our home, about sixty-five or seventy miles, so it was easy to get there. My older sister and my brother had both gone to school there, and so, naturally, they didn't want me to even think of going to any other college.

I had a really good professor at Utah State named Max Dalby. When I had attended the summer music camp before I started college, a professor from UCLA who taught at the camp every year had told me about Max, and I met him at the camp. Max was a musical genius.

Max was a big man, probably about six foot one, with very dark brown, almost black, piercing eyes. If you came to your lesson unprepared, he would just stop and look at you. You'd say, "That's enough. Just let me go to work on it, and I'll be back next week." He would stop a band and everyone would think, "Oh, no. What did he hear?" I learned from Max how to listen for specific things

The first time I played in a big jazz band was in 1958, at a music camp the summer before I started college at Utah State University.

when an entire band of a hundred pieces was playing and be able to say, "Okay, there's a wrong note in the third trumpet section. We've got to figure that out and get rid of it." He was tough, but he was good, and we became close friends.

Max took me under his wing, and I learned as much as I possibly could. Thanks to Max, when I started teaching, I'd already rehearsed bands—I knew what to do. I knew when I walked into rehearsal the very first day. There wasn't a doubt in my mind; I knew exactly what had to happen to help these kids. They trusted me and accepted my authority, and away we went.

Many years later, I sent Max an album featuring two musicians from the former Soviet Union playing my tunes. I received a rare phone call from him, and he told me he loved my music, and that he was proud of me. Coming from a man like Max, that really meant a lot.

I also had a wonderful professor named Al Wardle, who gave me private lessons on brass instruments. Every Saturday I'd go to his office and practice for three or four hours, and my father paid for the lessons with lamb meat. I got so good on various brass instruments that I played tuba in the faculty brass quartet when I was still working on my doctorate.

When I was an undergraduate from 1958 to 1962, there was no jazz program at the university level. You could be in a jazz band called the Scotsmen, but you didn't get any credit for it.

The band wasn't actually an official, school-sanctioned group. We rehearsed on campus and performed at various school functions, and we actually got paid. You couldn't take a class in jazz theory or jazz history or jazz anything. You just learned it by doing it.

The person who ran the Scotsmen was a man named Dick Beecher. He was teaching in the public schools, but he had a great ear, and he was a good piano player. I watched him carefully, and I learned everything I could from him about writing for piano—how to voice chords and so forth. I did my student teaching under him before I finished my degree, and that was a truly worthwhile and valuable experience.

This is me in 1959, when I was a
sophomore at Utah State University.

CHAPTER 10

Beginning My Musical Career with Elvon

THE FIRST TIME I SAW ELVON WAS ON THE NIGHT OF my eighth-grade graduation party. All the schools from the surrounding small towns graduated at the same time. My friend, Larry Grimes, and I were checking out these three girls from Geneva, Idaho. Elvon was one of them, and she was definitely the most beautiful of the three.

Elvon and I began attending Montpelier High School together later that year and gradually became friends. She was dating other people, but one of my friends suggested she might go with me to a school dance. She was sitting behind me in one of our classes, and I finally got up the nerve to pass her a note. That was a cool thing to do, if you didn't get caught. About two seconds

later, she sent back a note
that said, "I'd love to go with
you." I almost had to catch
my breath when I read it,
because she was the most
lovely young lady I had ever
seen in my life. She was full
of life and energy, and she
loved music.

Here's a shot of Elvon and
me early in our marriage.

Elvon had an incredible
ear for music. When I was
teaching in the public schools, if I asked her what she thought of
a band concert, she'd think about it for a minute, and then say
something like, "Well, you know, that ninth-grade band sounds
like it could use a little help." Or later, after a night at the jazz festival, I'd come home and say, "What did you think about that?"
And she'd say, "Oh, I loved it. The only thing I missed was being
able to sit with you and hold your hand." I hadn't been sitting
with her because I was off running the festival.

Elvon and I were dating when we went off to college, and
we got married two years later. In college, I played two or three
nights a week in my own jazz band. Elvon and I married when we
were nineteen, when we each had two years of college remaining,
but we were determined to finish. She went to school, I went to
school, and I kept playing music.

Being married and still in college wasn't the easiest thing for
either of us. Being a music major, I was in rehearsals a lot. I was also
in the university's big band, and was playing two or three nights a
week in my own band. Elvon often came to hear me play. Several
guys in the big band were married, and our wives often came to
our performances. After gigs we'd all go have a pizza or something.

Having my own band was the greatest experience for me,
because that's when I started playing piano seriously. The piano
pushed me in a new direction. It helped me better understand

the way music happened. We had a piano, bass, drums, and two saxophone players who could play all the woodwinds—any kind of sax, clarinet, flute, it didn't matter. We could play such a wide range of tunes that it was a kick every time we performed.

I played piano in my own band and saxophone and trombone in the big band. Both experiences really helped me get going in music. I had some incredible players in my small band—kids who knew a lot more about jazz than I did. Those guys really knew how to improvise, and I listened carefully, trying to learn from them.

I graduated from college in 1962 and was hired as the band director for the Rexburg-Madison School District. My goal was to be a music teacher in the public schools, although I didn't realize at the time that you could practically starve to death doing it. I really didn't think about that. Looking back, I probably should have. But at least I was well prepared to teach music.

There was a big reason for that: in college, my band director had made me promise I wouldn't touch the saxophone for a year. During that time I started to work on the clarinet, and by the end of the first year I had made my way up to first chair in the clarinet section. Then I started working on the flute, trombone, and

In 1962, at age twenty-one, I became the director of music for the Rexburg-Madison School District in southern Idaho.

tuba. After that, I took lessons on the French horn, oboe, and bassoon. I played the flute and the trombone quite well. I was trying to learn all the instruments as well as I could, so that when I got to the public schools and started to teach band, I would really be able to help the kids.

Right from the start, I had a summer school program. I would finish the school year, then teach a six-week summer band program that usually had about 130–140 kids who wanted to be in the band when school began in the fall. I'd get them started during the six-week summer band program, use the next six weeks to work some more on my master's degree, and then come back and start a new school year. My work just never stopped. From my first year on, there was never a break.

My rehearsals started at six thirty in the morning with the jazz band, and then I had section rehearsals. Sometimes I'd meet with students on Saturday mornings to make sure they were doing the right things, that they were learning all the right fingerings and everything. These kids were extremely committed. After five or six years, we were probably one of the best high school bands in the country. They just got into it—loving it because they were doing well. When you do well at something, you want to keep going with it.

The high school band really kept these kids interested, and it was a great experience for me. If they needed help, I could play the trombone parts, or I could probably play the second or third trumpet parts and do fine. I could play all the saxophone parts. I could play all the piano stuff, of course. We needed to work on style and sound, and I was able to really help them with that.

CHAPTER 11

Back to School

IN 1968, I'D BEEN TEACHING FOR SIX YEARS, AND I WAS in charge of a band program with 575 students. I had the elementary band, the junior high band, the high school program, the jazz band, and the high school pep band. The pep band performed at every football and basketball game, and I went with them. I was at the school from six in the morning until sometimes ten at night, as well as all day on Saturdays. On Sundays, I'd go back and make sure everything was ready to start again on Monday. After six years of that, I knew I was going to do myself in.

Max Dalby had judged a state band competition my band was in. He told me my band was fantastic, but that it looked like I could use a break.

He said, "I'm worried about you. I think you're going to kill yourself by working too hard." I had already earned my master's degree, and he said he wanted me to come back to Utah State and work on my doctorate for a couple of years. He said I'd be given an assistantship and I could teach some classes at the university while I was working on my degree. It sounded like a good deal to me, and I took it.

I had finished a third of my master's requirements before I even began teaching school in 1962. During the summers, after teaching band camp, I finished my master's degree in performance on piano, clarinet, flute, saxophone, trombone, euphonium, and bass clarinet. I played a different major work on each of these instruments in a single recital in 1967.

I decided to go for my doctorate in music theory, curriculum development, and supervision in music education.

In early January, the first year I was away from public school working on my doctorate, I got a call from the Rexburg-Madison Superintendent of Schools. He told me the man who had taken my place had left unexpectedly, and there was no one to lead the band program. He asked if I would come back. I promised him I would do whatever it took to keep the band program afloat—even quit school, if necessary.

It had been very difficult for me to turn that program over to someone else. My successor was a man I really trusted, but he ended up leaving because the pressure was too great with 575 kids a day. He just couldn't handle it. When I started to teach there in 1962, I was able to get the kids to really work hard for me because I had an incredible love for music and love for the young people.

I had told them, "Do you want to just be mediocre, or would you like to do something someone rarely does? If you want to do something someone rarely does, you're going to have to practice." I required five hours of practice a week to get an A in the sixth-grade band. By the time they got to high school, those kids had some chops. They could play anything.

For the rest of that school year, I was the band director again—but on a compressed schedule. I got up at four thirty in the morning on Fridays, and a friend and I went from Utah State University, in

Here I am with Elvon, my parents, Elvon's parents and my children Marc and Tera Lyn after I received my doctorate from Utah State University.

Logan, back to Rexburg, Idaho. I listened to every band and took notes on what was wrong and what needed to be done by the next week. I rehearsed those kids on Fridays and Saturdays and told them what they were doing wrong and what they had to do.

"We can fix it," they said. "We'll do it, we'll practice." So they would do their own rehearsing. Someone came and sat in the band room with them so things didn't get out of hand, but the students never gave anybody any trouble. They divided up in sectionals and went to work. When I came back the next week it was always amazing to see the progress they had made.

The next year, a friend of mine who had just finished his doctorate and wanted to get some experience in the public schools, took over the district's band program for a year. When I finished my degree, I went back to help again. That was probably one of the only school districts in the United States that had two PhD guys working with the band program. Then my friend got a job at Utah State University, and I was hired by the University of Idaho.

I finished my student teaching and was back at college at Utah State when I received a call from a band director with whom I had once student-taught at a junior high. He sounded terrible. He told me his band was getting ready for a big concert, and he was down with the flu. He asked if I would substitute teach for him while he recuperated.

I talked to all my professors, and they told me as long as I checked in with them, I could go ahead and do it. I was in all kinds of classes, but my professors were really great about it because they knew I was a little bit ahead on my program and that I only had one quarter left.

So I went to substitute teach at this high school, and the first day I was there, there was a kid who was just a smart aleck. He was a baritone player, and he gave me a lot of trouble—smart-mouthing and talking back to me. I had been about ready to send him to the principal's office, but I didn't know if that would do a whole lot of good. That night the teacher called and asked me how the first day had gone. I told him it had been fine, except for the student who had given me a hard time. He said, "I think everything will be okay tomorrow."

The next day the student met me at my car, and helped me bring in the music and set up the stands. During band, he was a model student. I was there for about ten days because the teacher was so sick, and this kid just really went to work. The night before the teacher came back, I told him how the student had straightened up and turned out to be such a big help. He told me he wasn't surprised. I asked him what he had done to cause the drastic change.

"I told him you won a Golden Gloves boxing championship."

CHAPTER 12

Jazz 101: Studying the Masters

IN 1962, WHEN I WAS TWENTY-ONE YEARS OLD, I started Idaho's first public school jazz band at Madison High School in Rexburg. They actually were called "stage bands" at that time. A big stage band movement was emerging, but it hadn't hit public schools much, and it certainly hadn't hit any schools in Idaho. So I went to the administrators and told them I'd like to start a stage band. They gave me permission and said if I kept track of attendance and all the typical paperwork, the students would get credit for it as a music class.

Those kids really got into it. They started to learn about style and did lots of listening. I about wore out my jazz records, but I didn't mind. The students were really listening and trying to learn about jazz, and it was a wonderful thing to see. That band went on to win several competitions in the late 1960s and early 1970s.

I started the first high school jazz band in Idaho in 1962. The students were genuinely interested in the foundations of jazz and seriously listened to and studied the jazz greats.

In my first year as festival director at the University of Idaho, I noticed that students who came to perform and be adjudicated had not had much contact with jazz, and it often showed in their performances. There were some good groups, of course, but many of the students clearly were not in touch with the music itself.

I would talk to these students and ask them, who's your favorite jazz trumpeter? Who's your favorite jazz pianist? Who's your favorite jazz whatever? And they couldn't even name one jazz artist. They just looked at me like, "I don't know, I don't ever listen." I told them they would never understand jazz until they went back and listened to the people who made it happen. They needed to do their homework. They needed to find out what made this music happen and study it.

If it was that bad here, where we had a jazz festival, I was concerned that, if somebody didn't do something, this music I loved so much could be lost.

The listening part is so important. When you say you're doing jazz, that means you have to understand chord structure, improvisation, different styles, and so on. You have to understand the many things that go into making jazz happen—and with these kids, that wasn't taking place. There were a few who knew about it, but overall the knowledge was very limited.

I felt like these students could have more experience in listening to the music if we added another day to the festival to allow university and college vocal and instrumental ensembles to perform. At the time, the University of Idaho jazz groups performed at the festival, but they didn't compete against other schools. I started talking to some of the college music directors from around the Northwest, and they agreed that adding another day would be a good thing. The "college day" was added in 1978, my second year of directing the festival.

I also felt the students needed to hear some of the great jazz artists, so during that second year, we had a special concert with vibes player Gary Burton and his quintet. I always thought it was interesting that our first concert had Gary—a vibes player who was a very close friend of Hamp's. Gary did a marvelous clinic on improvisation that was pretty well attended. However, most of the students had never attended a clinic or workshop before, so it was difficult for them to really appreciate it and get the full value of what was happening. But it was a start.

In 1982, Dianne Reeves—who has since won a number of Grammys and is a very dear friend—had just put out her first record, and her manager sent me a copy. I listened to it and thought, "Wow, she's really got it." So we invited her to the 1983 festival.

Right away, she said, "What I'd like to do is be involved with the students a little more. I'll do a clinic, but is there something else I could do?" That was one of the first years we had a solo vocal division, and she judged all the vocal solos on Friday. She probably wouldn't do that now, but what a great experience for the kids to work with her.

As we continued to bring the top-tier artists and offer clinics, the students and teachers who came to the festival started viewing it differently. It became a true jazz education experience.

Hamp and me at the 1990 festival in Moscow.

It was no longer just a place to go play your horn for twenty minutes and be judged. Now it was becoming a place not only to watch professional jazz artists perform, but also to hear them talk about what helped them get to where they were.

The clinics have always run about sixty to ninety minutes, but their purpose and format has always varied greatly. Some clinics are more like mini-concerts, others are a combination of music and lecture, and some are strictly lecture. Gerry Mulligan, the great baritone saxophonist, didn't play a note during his clinic in 1992, and instead gave a talk about the history of jazz. The jazz critic Leonard Feather gave clinics on jazz history each year from 1990 to 1994.

Even the biggest stars of the jazz world were moved by what they experienced in the clinics. The great guitarist Herb Ellis told me, "I've never had fifty guitar players at my feet, asking, 'What pick do you use?'" Dizzy Gillespie, who performed at the festival in 1988 and 1991, was overcome with emotion following his clinic in 1991, which was standing room only in the largest clinic space on campus, and even had students sitting on the stage. He

The Lionel Hampton Jazz Festival grew bigger and more popular every year during the 1990s. This photo from 1993 shows: (Back, l-r) Richard Hahn, Robert Spevacek, Myron Wahls, and me. (Front, l-r) Lee Etta Powell, UI President Elisabeth Zinser, and Hamp.

couldn't believe that young people knew who he was and were idolizing him like that.

Eventually, the clinics became so big we couldn't hold them in the School of Music building. We had to open up the Student Union Building—and even then we had overflow. We had to have people on hand to manage the large number of students who wanted to get into the clinics. We had to clear the place out like a movie theater so new kids could go in. The clinics just started getting packed.

In 1989, there were only eight clinics. By 1993, there were twenty-three, and by 1996 there were thirty-seven. Today there are more than a hundred clinics, workshops, and special exhibits during the festival.

The festival started to grow, and just about every artist from then on did a clinic. Now the clinics take place at numerous locations around campus and the community. It's been incredible to see that happen. Everywhere young people go on campus during the jazz festival there are artists who are grateful and honored to have the opportunity to pass along their love of jazz to another generation. Due to their intimate setting, the clinics are an especially ideal place to do that.

The only way you can learn about jazz is to first study the masters. So we brought the masters here for the students to study. Although we have lost many of

Me in 1990 with a rare mustache.

those jazz legends in the decades since the festival began, we have also started bringing in younger artists who have the same kinds of musical ideals. We tried so hard to instill in the minds of students that you need to study the jazz greats. If you don't do that, it isn't that you can't play, and it isn't that you can't do something great—but you don't have that background to fall back on, to have as your base to work from. When I see young players who are playing extremely well and who also have that background, it just makes my heart jump with joy. It's fresh, but it ties in to the thing that made it happen—the great jazz artists of the past.

That's why I decided we needed to change the way we were

doing things. Many students came to the festival from small towns throughout the Northwest. It was unlikely they would ever go to New York, Los Angeles, or some other big city to hear big-name jazz artists. That was a major problem, and I decided that if the students weren't likely to go to the artists, then we should bring the artists to the students. And if we were going to make a difference in the educational value of the festival, we needed to bring in the *finest* jazz artists.

I knew if we were going to do the festival, it had to be done right. It needed to grow. It needed to touch more kids. We were not going to bring in pop music and we were not going to bring in smooth jazz. It had to be traditional jazz, and it had to be the real deal. It was going to be the thing that had made it happen from the beginning. I knew we had to keep the roots of the music alive.

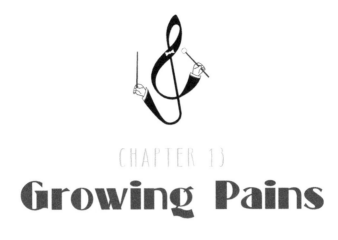

CHAPTER 13

Growing Pains

I DIDN'T HAVE ANY HELP WITH THE JAZZ FESTIVAL AT first, but eventually some students stepped forward, and that was a powerful learning experience for some of them.

I met all the judges and artists—picked them up from the airport, took them to their hotel rooms, and brought them to campus. I did everything I could to make sure they were comfortable and felt welcome. And there was really no one to help me because there was no budget for it. The only budget we had was the money we could make from the festival. Eventually, I had enough money to hire a graduate assistant, and for two years a young woman was my assistant as she worked on her master's degree. That worked out well, and we decided to hire her back on. It was a big change.

Eventually, I completely rewrote all the festival rules for every division. I felt there was a problem with the classifications, because schools of widely ranging sizes were in the same division.

I created a B division for schools with fewer than two hundred students, and that made a huge difference. The first year it was offered, I think there were two entries in that division, but as soon as schools found out about it, we had an entire division filled, and it was that way for years.

The other thing we changed was adding the college day. At that time, there was only Friday, which was for vocal competition, and Saturday, which was for instrumental and junior high and high school competition. The first year the festival was under my direction, the competitions remained the same, running for two days. Then I started talking to college music directors from Utah, Idaho, Washington, Oregon, and Montana. They said they liked the idea of having a college music day at the festival.

The reason we expanded to a four-day festival is that there were so many junior high and middle school kids attending that we were having trouble finding enough room for them to perform. To solve this problem, we decided to add a separate day for those grades.

Then I started to look at the junior high division, which also included elementary students. I remember one year a junior high choir lost to an elementary school choir, and some of the teachers went crazy about it. They felt the reason the elementary choir won was because the students were young and cute and so forth, though it was really because they did the best job of singing. To avoid that problem in the future, we added another division for just elementary students. There were probably two schools at first, but later there were more than fifty schools involved in elementary band and choir programs.

We were starting to get so many schools, and these junior high and middle school divisions were growing so rapidly we were having trouble keeping it the way I wanted it—that is, to not let it get so big that it was out of hand on any particular day. So in the 1990s, we moved all those schools to Wednesday, which became a special day just for junior high, middle school, and elementary kids. It made an incredible difference to them. They felt like they were not here with the college and high school kids, but instead had a day of their own.

When I first started working with the festival, our mailing list was very limited and included mainly schools in Washington, Idaho, Oregon, and maybe a few in Montana. Of course, in 1977, there was no such thing as the internet, but with a few phone calls, I found people who had fairly good lists that we could get.

In the fall of 1981 I had one of three very expensive computers on the UI campus. A dean had one, the President's office had one, and I had one for the festival. We also had a dot matrix printer—it was incredibly noisy, but we were grateful to have it. It had a dual disk drive, and there was only enough storage in the computer to do about seven or eight pages, and then you had to save it on a floppy disk.

A friend of mine from Idaho Falls was at the University of Idaho, working on his doctorate in computer technology, and he told me about a computer program that did just the kind of stuff I was doing—basically, keeping track of names. We used that program for years, and that was how I kept track of all the schools.

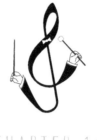

CHAPTER 14

A Very Important Question

AFTER THE 1984 FESTIVAL, I STARTED DOING SOME research and discovered there had never been a festival anywhere in the world named after a jazz artist. So I made an appointment with University of Idaho president Richard Gibb, who had really enjoyed meeting Hamp.

Dr. Gibb was an agricultural specialist, but what he had seen happen with the festival had really touched him—having Hamp perform, having Ella Fitzgerald perform, seeing the festival start to grow. I asked him if he thought it would be possible to rename the jazz festival in honor of Hamp, making it the world's first jazz festival to be named after a jazz artist. Not only did I get his permission, but his blessing as well.

Hamp was on the road somewhere, so I found out where he was staying and called his hotel. His valet answered the phone, and when I asked for Hamp, I was told he was resting. I could hear Hamp in the background saying, "Who's that on the phone?" The valet said, "It's Doc Skinner. He wants to ask you something." When Hamp picked up the phone, I said, "Mr. Hampton, I have a very important question to ask you."

I told him what the university wanted to do, and he said, "Oh, man, would I ever love that! This is going to happen?" I said, "Yes, I just needed your permission." He immediately started talking about the next festival, the one that would have his name on it. "Who would you like to have, Doc? How about Hank Jones? Would you like to have Stan Getz?"

I said, "Are you kidding me?"

I was in New York in the summer of 1985, and a friend who was then the vice president of the Manhattan School of Music handed me a *New York Times* article about the festival. She said, "Do you have any idea how much any of us would give to have an article like this in the *New York Times*?"

That 1985 festival was really a kick. Not only did media from around the world help pay tribute to Hamp, but the prior November Hamp had promoted the upcoming festival during an appearance on "The Today Show."

After Hamp's trio played, they interviewed Hamp, and he really talked up the festival. I started getting phone calls from people who wanted to learn more about it. All of a sudden, student groups from all over the place wanted to come and be a part of it. Hamp was ecstatic about what we had done.

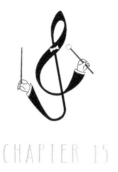

CHAPTER 15

Hank, Stan, and Ray

IN 1985, HANK JONES WAS CONSIDERED BY MANY TO BE one of the best jazz pianists in the world, and here was Hamp, saying, "How would you like his trio to come and be the house group?" That just blew me away. I got to know Hank Jones through Hamp, and we developed a very close relationship.

Then Hamp gave me Stan Getz's home phone number and told me to call him and invite him to the festival.

I had been listening to Stan Getz's recordings since I was a kid. He was an absolute legend in the world of jazz, and I was about to call him on the phone.

I managed to gather myself together by the time he answered, and I said, "Mr. Getz, you don't know me from Adam, but here's what's happening. We're going to rename the Idaho Jazz Festival the Lionel Hampton Jazz Festival, and Lionel Hampton would like you to be at the very first festival with his name on it."

Stan, who had recorded the album *Hamp and Getz* with Hamp

I always enjoyed the opportunity to perform with Hamp's band.

in 1955, told me he had never forgotten what he'd learned about timing and rhythm from Hamp on that recording session. He said, "There's nothing in the world I'd rather do than come and be with Hamp. You just tell me what I need to do, and I'll be there."

About six weeks before the 1985 festival, Hank Jones called to tell me his bass player was sick, and that he didn't see him making the festival in Moscow.

Then he said, "I do have a replacement, if it's okay with you, Doc." He said he was a very close friend, and they had played a lot together.

"Well, who is it?" I asked.

"Ray Brown."

So for the 1985 festival we changed some posters so we could get Ray Brown's name on them. Ray Brown was coming to the festival, and heads were spinning again. Ray was incredible, and we became very close friends. We talked on the phone at least once a week, until his untimely death in July 2002.

In addition to the Hank Jones Trio, the 1985 festival featured Slide Hampton and Anita O'Day. Also, instead of flying Hamp's big band out from New York, we put together something called the All-Northwest Pro Big Band. I played second tenor, and Hamp worked us just as he worked all his bands.

The bass player was a University of Idaho student. He was a great player, but he was young. During the performance, Hamp was playing away and he seemed to forget he wasn't with his own

Enjoying a laugh with Ray Brown.

big band and that these younger musicians might not know the tunes, and he just started calling all these tunes. I'd been worried that would happen, but somehow everybody hung in there with him to the end.

Before he left the stage, Hamp said, "I want to do something with just the bass player, the piano player, and Stan Getz." The bass player came out, and I think he was scared to death, but he hung in and did a great job. He's now playing professionally, probably partly because of that one experience with Hamp. Having a high regard for young musicians was just Hamp's way of doing things.

After the festival, someone called and told me Stan was in his motel room, and he wasn't going to leave until I came to see him. When I got there, he gave me a hug and said, "Doc, thanks for all you've done for Hamp, and thank you for what you've done for all of us in jazz." Stan became a very close friend of mine. He'd call me every two or three months to see how things were going. He knew I loved him unconditionally.

Stan came to the festival again in 1989. Shortly before the festival, he called me and said, "I don't think I'm going to be able to come, Doc. Someone slipped me a drink on New Year's Eve, and I fell off the wagon." I said, "Do you feel like you can't play?" and he said, "No."

I said, "Well, I've already got the word out that you're going to be here, buddy. I don't know what to do. I don't want to have to go to the newspaper and say, 'Sorry, folks. Stan Getz isn't going to be here.'" I told him I'd be willing to help him any way I could. Finally, he said, "You know, Doc, you'd make a hell of an attorney, and I'd like to hire you to be mine. You just convinced me that's what I should do."

Stan played on Friday night of the 1989 festival. He had just listened to two performers from the former Soviet Union do their first tunes, and he was standing backstage by his dressing room with tears running down his face. I walked up to him and gave him a hug, and he told me seeing those musicians brought back some incredible feelings. He asked me if I knew his parents had come to the US from Russia. Then he told me he had liver cancer and that his time was limited. I will never forget that special moment. He died later that year.

It was remarkable seeing the way Stan played, knowing he had cancer, and that his health was so bad. I've seen photos of him from that concert—he's looking at Hamp in a way that would tear your heart out. Right up until he died, I talked with him every few months on the phone. There are all kinds of stories about how Stan Getz often lost his cool, but never once did he lose it with me. My experience with him was extremely positive.

It was always special to watch Hamp interact with the artists and the audience. He knew how to reach everyone. He ran

It was one of the thrills of my life to get to know Hank Jones through the Lionel Hampton Jazz Festival.

the rehearsals and sound checks—and with Hamp, sound checks were practically like rehearsals.

As we walked off the stage from the first Lionel Hampton Jazz Festival concert in 1985, Hamp was already asking what artists I would like to have for the festival the following year. We started to talk nearly every day. We were becoming close friends. Hamp believed in me, and I truly loved him as my brother.

CHAPTER 16

A Tribute to Jazz Itself

SARAH VAUGHAN WAS VERY PROUD OF THE FESTIVAL being named in honor of her friend. She wanted to come back one more time to perform with Hamp, but she had cancer. I talked to her manager, and he was very kind, but he told me Sarah was not strong enough to perform. Later, I was told Sarah's last words were, "I just wanted to perform once more with Hamp at his jazz festival in Idaho."

In the coming years, Hamp would call me at home—sometimes at two thirty or three in the morning—full of excitement and energy, bursting with ideas about the festival and performers he wanted to bring in. It was amazing to see how he was so connected to the whole jazz network.

When the festival was named for Lionel Hampton, the jazz world and jazz artists felt that for someone to finally name a festival for a jazz artist was not just a tribute to Lionel Hampton—it was a tribute to jazz itself. For a university to have a festival named for a jazz artist was a big-time change. When I was going to school at Utah State University in the late 1950s and early 1960s, it was almost like jazz had a bad name. In those days, a lot of us learned about jazz by playing and listening to it together. You couldn't even take a class in it. You could do the jazz band, but couldn't get credit for it. You tried out, you were in it, but there was no credit. So what we did at the University of Idaho was really a major change in how people looked at jazz education and the importance of jazz.

The great tenor sax player Jimmy Heath received a Lionel Hampton Jazz Hall of Fame Award in 1988.

To students, I think the Lionel Hampton Jazz Festival says this music is valuable enough that a place has been created where the greatest artists in the world come to help make a difference in the lives of young musicians. The festival changed the lives of thousands and thousands of people. The students who came to the festival started to understand music's power to elevate the soul to new heights—a power that we don't even understand. That was Hamp's life. It is my life. That's why I think we had such an incredible friendship. We both understood the power of music. We loved the music, and we loved the people who created it.

Hamp took an active role in the festival right from the start, and the list of artists he introduced to the festival over the years is astounding: Ray Brown, Milt Hinton, Dizzy Gillespie, Gerry Mulligan, Ernestine Anderson, Betty Carter, Jon Faddis, Wynton Marsalis, Branford Marsalis, Carmen McRae, Benny Golson, Art Farmer, Al Grey, Pete and Conte Candoli, Terence Blanchard, Clark Terry, Wallace Roney, Freddie Hubbard, Tommy Flanagan, Kenny Barron, Cedar Walton, George Mraz, and many, many more. (See Chapter 34 for a more complete list.)

The student competitions and the artist's workshops expanded and took on new meaning. Later, our Jazz in the Schools program began introducing world-class jazz to elementary school students throughout the region. Hamp also took an active role in developing scholarships to the university's music school.

Hamp and I talked frequently—often about the festival, but as we became friends, we also discussed our families, lives, and hopes. His passion for education—for developing talent in others—kept coming through.

In January 1997, there was a fire in Hamp's New York City apartment. My experience with him after that is a great example of his selfless and giving personality. He was eighty-eight at the time. He called me from outside the building, as he sat in his wheelchair in his pajamas and robe, watching flames shooting out the windows of his apartment on the twenty-eighth floor, which overlooked Broadway and Lincoln Center. He had suffered two strokes in 1995, and had been helped out of his apartment by two assistants.

The first thing he said to me was, "Doc, are you okay?" Of course, I didn't know anything about the fire, so I answered, "I'm doing great. How are you?"

Then he told me what was happening.

"My apartment's on fire, Doc. I can see flames shooting out of my apartment. I don't know what happened."

He told me he was safe, but that everything was gone—his music, vibes, piano, drums, memorabilia, clothing.

Here's a photo of Hank Jones and me from the early 1990s.

"Everything I own is gone except this pair of pajamas and robe."

I told him not everything was gone.

"What do you mean, Doc?"

"You still have all of us, who love you so much."

He immediately brightened up and said, "Oh, you're right about that, Doc!"

He told me that he wanted me to hear about the fire from him, because the major networks were there filming the whole thing. He said he would be staying nearby until his apartment was fixed, and that he'd call again when he had settled in. Then he came to what was apparently the real reason for his phone call.

"This thing's been hitting the news, Doc. There are cameras from CBS and NBC and ABC. I can see them everyplace. It's going to be on the national news."

Student Valarie Harris performed a song for Hamp at a festival in the mid-90s and blew everyone away.

Then, sitting there at the curb in his wheelchair on that winter morning, his belongings literally going up in smoke before his eyes, Hamp said, "The fire isn't all bad, Doc."

"What do you mean?" I asked.

"We're getting some good publicity!"

Not long after that, Hamp called and told me he was really missing his piano. I called my friend, Tom Bunker, with the Kurzweil piano company, and told him Hamp needed a piano because his had been lost in the fire. A few minutes later Tom called back and asked for Hamp's address, and a new Kurzweil digital piano was delivered to Hamp the next day.

Just a couple days after that, Hamp was awarded the National Medal of Arts by President Bill Clinton.

CHAPTER 17

Dizzy, Delayed

AS THE 1986 FESTIVAL APPROACHED, WE WERE SELLING tickets like crazy, and I got a phone call from the university's safety office. I was told we could only sell 1,800 tickets for the concert in Memorial Gym. We had already sold more than that for the Dizzy Gillespie concert, so we had to announce that the concert was sold out. I called President Gibb's office and told him of the problem, and he gave permission to sell 500 more tickets. We made an announcement on a local radio station, and the tickets were sold in less than fifteen minutes.

Dizzy was supposed to perform on Saturday evening of the festival, but on Saturday morning I got a phone call from someone in Dizzy Gillespie's office informing me Dizzy would not be able to come to the festival. He'd recently had some kind of eye surgery, and his doctors were concerned that the strain of playing his trumpet could damage his eyes. We were very sorry to hear that, but realized Dizzy's well-being was most important.

I wish I could remember this young man's name, but he was from Boise, and he was the first winner of the solo instrumental competition in 1986. After he was awarded the trumpet, Hamp asked him to perform with him onstage.

When Hamp announced from the stage that Dizzy wasn't going to be at the festival that year, but that the audience was about to get the treat of a lifetime, he meant it. The band played at a new level, and Dianne Reeves came out and sang two tunes that knocked everyone off their chairs. As they had done the first time Hamp appeared at the festival, the band went out into the audience and played, and the kids followed them around. It was a show to behold. We also had Illinois Jacquet, Pete and Conte Candoli, and the Ray Brown Trio with Gene Harris and Mickey Roker. Clare Bathé was part of the Thursday evening concert, which was held in the Student Union Ballroom. The other concerts were in Memorial Gym.

Mickey Roker sang dirty limericks—about me—all the way up the stairs of Memorial Gym, and Ray Brown was laughing his head off. That was also the first year Ray's band was the house trio. Clare Bathé's performance was warm and exciting. When she sang "Send in the Clowns," I don't think there was a dry eye in the audience.

Also, the 1986 festival was the first year we had the solo instrumental division. That first year, it was only open to high school students. There were just a few students in it, but later there would be hundreds. A company had donated a really nice trumpet to give as a prize for the top soloist. Fortunately, the student who won it was a trumpet player from Boise. It would have been a bummer to give that trumpet to a saxophone player! Hamp wanted us to present the horn to the student at the concert. We called him up, and the kids stood and cheered. We handed him that beautiful horn, and he just stood there looking at it. Then Hamp said, "How would you like to play some blues with my band?"

Hamp, Gene Harris, Ray Brown, me, and Mickey Roker, in 1986.

The kid got through the tune with the band. I don't know that he always played everything exactly right, but those kids loved it. They stood up and cheered for him, and Hamp gave the kid a big hug. I think that changed that student's life. He became a music major, and a professional trumpet player—and he's still playing today, as far as I know.

When I started directing the festival, I was disappointed to see that probably fewer than a hundred kids were attending the early evening concert featuring the winning students. So the next year I started giving speeches. I told them they were at the festival to listen—and that included listening to their fellow students who had worked so hard and been given the honor to play. I said they should respect the students' accomplishments and perhaps even be inspired by them.

Here's a shot of Hamp and me at the 1986 festival.

After that first speech, something happened. The students started to stay. By the 2000s, we had five or six thousand kids in the Kibbie Dome for that early concert. It was the most amazing thing. All these kids were there to support the people who had been chosen to play. They would listen to them and say, "Maybe I could do a little better." Listening to those winning students really inspired a lot of the other students, and then it wasn't always the same ones on that stage.

CHAPTER 18

Moving to the Dome, and a Visit from an Old Friend

THE LAST CONCERTS IN MEMORIAL GYM WERE IN 1986, when we realized audiences were growing too large for the space. After that year's festival, I met with the president of the university, and he said we needed to figure out how to have concerts in the Kibbie Dome.

The Kibbie Dome, which I believe then seated eight thousand, is a scary building to look at when you're onstage, but when it's filled with sound, correctly, it is a great place to perform and listen to music. When we made the decision to move the concerts to the Kibbie Dome, the university brought in sound specialists. They fired blanks to determine how big the sound had to be to reach the back wall without reverberating. They determined the best place to put the stage and spent more than a week testing music and various sounds, to see what it took to fill the building. For several years, beginning in 1988, a company affiliated with the National Association of Music Merchants provided all the soundboards for the festival. These were $250,000 pieces of equipment. The university eventually bought one of its own, because football and basketball games were played in the Dome as well, and a good sound system was necessary. The quality of the sound was a big thing for me, if we were going to have concerts in the Dome.

In the summer of 1987, the year the music school was renamed, an old friend of mine from high school named Bob Wiggington pulled up to my house in a big Lincoln Continental. He told me he was the new head of Kawai America, and that he wanted me to come to the next National Association of Music Merchants show with him.

I went to the show that fall, and Bob introduced me to representatives of various instrument companies. Pretty soon I had drum sets, bass guitars, amplifiers, cymbal sets, saxophones— everything but bassoons and oboes. I continued going on my own after that first year. I'd approach the vendors and say, "I work for the Lionel Hampton Jazz Festival," and then explain a little about the purpose of the festival.

I told them I was trying to make a difference in the lives of students, who I wanted to do their very best. It's impossible to know if someone has talent unless they go to work. I've seen that with my own students. The ones who focus and apply themselves rise to the top.

Seeing my passion for the students and for music education convinced vendors to donate musical instruments. At one time I probably had three or four hundred thousand dollars' worth of instruments donated by companies that wanted to support the festival. Every student who won a competition at the festival knew they would receive a very nice prize.

CHAPTER 19

Expecting
Something Different

Hamp and me at a festival sound check in the mid-1990s.

WHEN HAMP SIGNED autographs, he often added comments like, "God loves you and so do I." He really did love people. That's the way I've always felt, too, so Hamp and I worked well together. When artists got to the festival they knew that they would be cared for and appreciated. I could talk to them, not just about them as people, but about their music, about their recordings, about what they were doing on the stage.

78

We booked groups of musicians who had never played together before. Some of the people who hooked up with each other at the festival later recorded and toured together. Artists felt like the festival was a home. They felt like they had some ownership in it, like they were part of the legacy. That was what made the festival so special, year after year.

I think the success of the festival was because of that mixture of music. It's the mix, the friendships, the people loving one another and caring deeply about what was happening at the festival. It's because of that mixture that the magic keeps happening. The greatest thing I saw was that when the artists came, they expected something different to happen than happened anywhere else.

Bill Watrous and I enjoy a moment with Hamp at the festival in the mid-1990s.

One year we had five guitarists at the festival—Bucky and John Pizzarelli, Russell Malone, Corey Christiansen, and a young guitarist from Oregon named John Stowell. They played together, putting on a show I don't think anyone could have anticipated. Other years, we did that with trumpets and trombones.

For many years, beginning around 1990, there was a performance before the Saturday night finale concert where all the student trombone players joined UI trombone professor Al Gemberling and other trombone professionals and teachers. Sometimes there were as many as 120 trombonists on stage. We called it the Big Bones Band. The group played three tunes, and they literally filled that huge Kibbie Dome with sound. The

Marlena Shaw performed at the festival in the early 1990s.

Here I am having a laugh with vocalist Evelyn White at her first appearance at the festival in 1998. Later that year, we did a ten-concert jazz tour in Russia.

performance was meant to fill time before the eight o'clock main concert, but it got to be where people wanted to be there early so they didn't miss that trombone group. We did that for more than a dozen years, and a lot of really fine trombonists took part in it. We had shirts made up for all the participants, and sometimes even the trombonists in Hamp's big band would join in.

CHAPTER 20

Nothing Like It in the World

SOMETIMES THE MOST DIFFICULT THING IN THE world is to become known in your own community. In 2007, I knew of probably a few hundred people from the Moscow area who attended the festival for the first time. One of these people I had known for years. She was a country-western music fan, but she told me the jazz festival was the most incredible thing she had ever been to in her life. I've seen that happen time after time. People attend for the first time and come away saying, "I had no idea."

The hardest thing is convincing people to take that first step—to take their family and go and have that experience. In all honesty, if you brought someone in from New York or England or Germany or France or Russia or Australia or New Zealand or California, anyplace but right at home, they'd be saying, there's nothing like it in the world. Ray Brown used to say to me every

Lou Rawls was always a hit at the festival. He first performed there in 1999.

year in the early 1990s, "Doc, this concert is $150 a pop in New York for the cheap seats!" And then he'd say, "But I don't think you'd ever be able to get this crew together anyplace else but right here." That's powerful.

After Hamp got involved, word about the festival started getting out to more jazz artists. He started talking to his friends. Al Grey started talking. Ray Brown started talking. Jeff Hamilton started talking. James Moody, Stanley Turrentine, Carmen McRae—they all talked about the festival. In 1994, the great jazz writer Leonard Feather called it the world's number one jazz festival, and his column had a big impact, because everyone trusted his word on jazz. People started calling, and it never stopped.

There are probably several reasons why the festival became so popular with students. The first is that there was not another

In the mid-1990s, jazz writer Leonard Feather, shown here
with Hamp and me in 1991, called the Lionel Hampton Jazz
Festival the number one jazz festival in the world.

Drummer Jeff Hamilton performed at the festival
several times, beginning in the mid-1990s.

Here I am with manager Larry Clothier, vocalist Roberta Gambarini, and pianist Tamir Hendelman in 2007.

thing like it anywhere in the world. These students could go to New York, San Francisco, Las Vegas, Paris, or anywhere, and if they stayed for a month they couldn't see all the artists who came to Moscow, Idaho, over a four-day period during the festival. (The festival was cut back to a two-day event a few years ago.) And at the festival, not only do they get to watch these artists perform— they get to rub shoulders with them in clinics and workshops. Just think of the opportunity these students have.

It's incredible to think of the legendary artists who have performed at the festival over the years: Hamp himself, Dizzy Gillespie, Tommy Flanagan, Gene Harris, Art Farmer, Benny Golson, Clark Terry, Ray Brown, Milt Hinton, and Al Grey. We've had Wallace Roney, Shirley Horn, Bucky Pizzarelli, Kenny Barron, Jeff Hamilton, Terence Blanchard, Paquito D'Rivera, Ernie Andrews, Roy Hargrove, Hank Jones, Joe Morello, Diana Krall, Al Jarreau, Lou Rawls, Dee Daniels, Elvin Jones—the list goes on and on.

The great trumpeter Roy Hargrove performed more than half a dozen times at the Lionel Hampton Jazz Festival, beginning in the mid-1990s.

Wynton Marsalis might never have come to the festival if not for Hamp. We had Wynton's brother, Delfeayo, at the festival before hardly anyone knew who he was—before he had even really started to play professionally.

There are artists who perform at the festival with musicians they've never met, and the next thing you know, they're recording and touring together. That's what happened to Roberta Gambarini, a singer I consider to be one of the greatest vocalists since Ella Fitzgerald and Sarah Vaughan. She met Hank Jones at the festival, he played for her for the first time, and then they performed and recorded together for years.

When pianist Marian McPartland came to the festival in 1995, she didn't know who her drummer would be. We had in mind a nineteen-year-old drummer from New Orleans named Brian Blade. Hamp had heard him and thought he was incredible and wanted him to be the house drummer for the festival.

Now, Marian was pretty particular about who played drums for her, but I told her Hamp thought Brian was really something. Brian was playing when I brought Marian into the Kibbie Dome for her sound check, and as we walked toward the stage she could hear him. She reached up, put her arms around my neck, pulled me down, and gave me a kiss on the cheek, saying,

"He's the one I've been looking for, Doc." After that, Marian and Brian performed together many times.

Marian called Hamp up to join her during her performance that night, and when he came off the stage, he told me it was one of the greatest experiences of his life. Later Marian and Hamp recorded a segment for Marian's public radio program, "Piano Jazz."

The University of Idaho's school of music was renamed the Lionel Hampton School of Music on February 28, 1987. It is the first and only music school named after a jazz artist and an African American.

CHAPTER 21

Lionel Hampton's School of Music

A FEW OF US IN THE SCHOOL OF MUSIC STARTED thinking about what had happened when the festival was renamed in honor of Lionel Hampton—especially the notoriety that followed. The festival had almost doubled in size in just a couple of years. We decided it would be a good idea to ask that the university's school of music itself be renamed for Lionel Hampton. The University of Idaho would have the first and only school of music in the world ever named after a jazz artist, and an African American.

The president of the University of Idaho, who had become a close friend of mine, was excited about the festival, so every once in a while he'd call me up to his office and we'd talk about how things were going. I also knew the provost extremely well. I had given him a limited edition festival poster that Hamp had signed.

The University of Idaho was launching the fundraising campaign for its hundredth birthday, which was coming up in 1989. Kirk Sullivan, vice president of Boise Cascade, had been assigned by the company to help the university with its fundraising efforts. Boise Cascade is a multibillion-dollar wood products and building materials company, and one of the biggest companies in Idaho. Kirk had access to a jet any time he wanted—whether he had to get to a meeting in Washington, DC, or wherever. One phone call, and thirty minutes later he was sitting in Moscow in a meeting with the president of the University of Idaho.

The president introduced me to Kirk, and when I told him about the festival, he said, "My wife and I want to come next

This is a photo from a press conference in Moscow in 1987, the year the UI school of music was named for Lionel Hampton. The other artists with Hamp are Ray Brown, Stanley Turrentine and Dianne Reeves.

year." We talked some more, and I said something needed to happen to change the national exposure for the University of Idaho. Then I thought, *Do I dare tell him, or not?*

So I told Kirk some people in the school of music had been talking about the idea of renaming the music school the Lionel Hampton School of Music. I reminded him we already had the first jazz festival in the world named after a jazz artist and an African American, and now we could be the first school of music with that same distinction. His eyes opened wide, and he looked at me and said, "This needs to happen."

So the president did what he needed to do. It was approved by the State Board of Education, but it was kept quiet so we could announce it during the following year's festival, and few people knew anything about it. I had a couple of people working in my office in the school of music who knew what was going on, but they never told a soul.

One day the University of Idaho president called and told me he and I were going to Washington, DC, to meet with Lionel Hampton and Kirk Sullivan. This still hadn't hit the press. People in our community didn't even know what was about to happen.

When we got to Washington, Kirk said, "Good news. I have a meeting set up with Vice President George Bush. He's a very close friend of Hamp's."

So we went to the Capitol Building and got the security clearance you need, and we were picked up. Pretty soon out comes George Bush, and he says, jokingly, "Okay, I want all the security people in the state here, these are friends of mine. Bring them in." It was senators and representatives from Idaho, Kirk Sullivan, the president of the University of Idaho, Vice President Bush, and myself. I still have an autographed photograph of me with the vice president.

Bush talked about his upbringing, and tears were rolling down his face. He said it was one of the most important things our country could do—to name a jazz festival and a university

University of Idaho music educators often got the chance to perform with Lionel Hampton. This is a shot of UI music professor Robert Miller and me playing with Hamp in 1987.

school of music after an African American. We wanted him come to Idaho for the renaming ceremony, but his schedule wouldn't allow it. Instead, he recorded a video message that we played at the ceremony. Hamp didn't know about the video, and he was quite surprised and pleased when he saw it.

After we had met with Vice President Bush, we met with Hamp, because Mr. Bush had meetings scheduled with President Reagan all night. I remember Hamp had a big badge he carried in his pocket; he could walk into the White House any time he wanted. It was an incredible thing that he was trusted so much by presidents. It didn't matter what party, he was always welcome there. In fact, during his seventy-five-year career, Hamp performed for every president from Harry S. Truman to George W. Bush.

When we got back to Idaho, I called Hamp and asked him, "Now, everything's okay?" And he said, "Oh, yeah. This is exactly what I want. This is my dream come true."

Then the university president reminded us we hadn't even informed the school of music faculty about what was happening. So he called a meeting of the music faculty. I think that may have been the first time a UI president had come to a faculty meeting.

He told us the University of Idaho had an incredible opportunity, and that renaming the school of music in honor of Lionel Hampton could be one of the most important things the university could ever do. He said the change wouldn't affect curriculum or anything the school was doing, but it would change the image of the university and give it national exposure. The faculty voted,

A joyful Hamp and myself at the 1987 festival.

and there was not a single opposing vote. There were a lot of questions at first, but there was not one dissenting vote.

Then it hit the press. As I said, it was the start of the university's fundraising campaign; all sorts of things were happening in regard to that, and then there was this national exposure about renaming the music school. I started getting phone calls from all over the country and from around the world.

The University of Idaho School of Music was renamed in Hamp's honor on February 28, 1987, at two in the afternoon. Two hours later, Hamp played a private concert for his school's faculty. That was a busy day for Hamp. I don't know how he found the energy to do it all, but he was so excited about having the school named after him. He said it was the greatest honor he'd ever received in his life.

Renaming the festival and the school of music brought a lot of acclaim to the university. When you can say, "I graduated from the Lionel Hampton School of Music," that means something special. Hamp meant quality.

I used to hear from people all the time who ran across professional musicians who had played at the festival as students. A man from Los Angeles told me he heard some young people performing at a little jazz club there called the Jazz Bakery. He went up to them to compliment them on their playing, and one of them told him, "We won the college division at the Lionel Hampton Jazz Festival, and here we are out on the road!"

CHAPTER 22

From Russia, with Jazz

JAZZ IS INTERNATIONAL MUSIC. EVEN THOUGH ITS roots are in the United States, it's all over the world and has been for many years. Many of the countries where American jazz artists play probably have ten times the jazz fans we have in the United States.

For six years, under my direction, the Lionel Hampton Jazz Festival was involved with the Library of Congress to bring budding young artists from Russia to the United States, where they could learn from the masters of jazz. I started the first Jazz in the Schools program in the United States, and I took my Russian artists to the schools.

In 1989, the Lionel Hampton Jazz Festival brought two artists from the Soviet Union as special guests. Saxophonist Lembit Saarsalu was from Estonia, and pianist Leonid Vintskevich was

This was the first time I met Lembit Saarsulu. He first came to the festival in 1989, along with Leonid Vintskevich, marking the first time musicians from the Soviet Union performed at the festival.

from Russia. We were told to say that they were from the Soviet Union, not Estonia or Russia. The musicians had a Soviet journalist named Alexey Batashev with them—he spoke English and was very helpful in getting them here. It seemed like Lembit and Leonid spoke little English except for the word "wonderful." Lembit spoke German very well, and I spoke it a little, so that was how we communicated. Leonid spoke only Russian, so Alexey acted as translator. Igor Butman, a Russian-born saxophonist who had become a US citizen a couple of years earlier, also performed at the festival that year.

This was the first year for a Wednesday concert, and Hamp had invited the opera star Patricia Miller to perform. Hamp had called me on Christmas Eve to tell me about Patricia, whom he'd heard the night before. Hamp invited her to the festival, and during her concert he accompanied her on vibes as she sang "Summertime."

At the 1989 festival, Lembit and Leonid knelt to pay tribute to Carmen McRae after her performance. She later asked me if they really knew who she was, and I told her they had probably heard everything she'd ever recorded—through either the black market or Radio Free Europe. I introduced them later, and she told them how much she had enjoyed their performances.

Pete Candoli, Igor Butman, Bill Watrous and John Clayton.

Leonid had played a Russian piece in a jazz idiom, and Lembit did the same with an Estonian folk tune that had an unbelievably beautiful melody. They took those original melodies but improvised with them and played them in the jazz style.

I've never seen anyone put as much energy into a slow ballad as Igor Butman. I thought we'd have to get some ice to cool off the stage after he played his first solo. But then Leonid played the most beautiful melodic line to kind of contrast what Igor had played. In their heads, their count-offs were in different languages, but when they got on stage, jazz became their language.

Lembit, Leonid, and I went down to Salmon, Idaho, after the festival to play a concert. It was a small venue, but it was jammed full of people, and Lembit and Leonid really got into it. One of them said, "I don't speak very good English, but I speak very good jazz!" That's the international language. That's the music talking, and it doesn't matter where you come from.

The 1989 festival was also special because we were able to

Russian-born horn player Arkady Schilkloper first performed
at the Lionel Hampton Jazz Festival in 1990. I call him the
best jazz French horn player on the planet.

bring in Wynton Marsalis. Prior to the festival, Wynton called
me and said he wanted to do a clinic. "Is there any way you can
set it up? I know my contract doesn't say it, but I'd love to do a
clinic with the kids." I promised him I'd have a room full of kids
for him. We announced it, it was packed, and the university was
tickled about it.

I'll never forget Wynton onstage that year. He was playing
with the Ray Brown Trio, which was Ray Brown, Jeff Hamilton on
drums, and Gene Harris on piano. Then they called Hamp up to
the stage. I think Ray was scheduled to play three or four tunes,
and then Hamp came up, and they added another five or six.

They had finished the first tune, one of Hamp's specials, and
for the second number, Hamp called the famous old tune "It

Might as Well Be Spring." Wynton didn't know the tune, and Ray Brown stood there giving hand signals to tell Wynton the chord progression and Wynton improvised behind it. They got through it just fine, and it was a wonderful thing to see.

When Wynton came off the stage, he came over and put his arm around me, and I said, "I just wanted to thank you for being willing to do that clinic with the kids. I think it really made a big difference." And Wynton said, "Well, let me tell you, Doc, the clinic happened tonight on that stage. That was the real clinic. Lionel Hampton was in charge, and he wasn't messing around."

When Hamp arrived at the Spokane airport for the festival that year, I found out he had traded in his first-class ticket for a coach ticket, and that the difference had come back to the festival. I've never seen an artist not fly first-class, but he wanted to

The Ukrainian vocal jazz group ManSound, which has a similar sound to the American vocal group Take 6, first performed at the Lionel Hampton Jazz Festival in 2000.

do it. In fact, Hamp paid Wynton's fee to perform at the festival. It was a gift to the festival and to the University of Idaho.

The 1989 festival had a lineup you just couldn't imagine, and as the festival grew and continued bringing in big-name artists, it was almost like there was nothing that could stop it. I could call about anywhere in the world and say, "We're interested in having so-and-so at the festival." Once in a while the cost was prohibitive, but many times they'd say, "They want to be there, Doc. What's it going to take to do it? How much do you have in your budget?" I'll bet that 95 percent of the time the artists said, "We'll do it for that price because we believe in what you're doing."

I've always felt that if we have the finest talent, then it doesn't really matter if you are black or white or whatever. To have Ella Fitzgerald here, to have Sarah Vaughan, to have Lionel Hampton. This, in spite of all the stuff that was going on up in northern Idaho for a while with groups like the Aryan Nations. I never had one artist ever say to me, "Doc, are we safe?"

I just think that goes to show that when you do the right thing for the right reasons, it will work out. We didn't name the festival for Lionel Hampton because he had money. I didn't even know he did, and that didn't make any difference anyway. My friendship with Lionel Hampton was true, honest, open, and real. He knew he had a friend here who he could say anything to. He knew I loved him like a brother, and that it was unconditional love. It was the same with the other artists who came to the festival.

Artists started saying, "Let us know when you want us back. We'll be there." People all over the world were reading about how all these great artists were coming to Idaho, and about how we were the first jazz festival and the only school of music to be named after a jazz artist and an African American. It was happening right here in Moscow, Idaho. It was out of love for the music and love for the artists. Naming the festival and the school of music after a jazz artist made all the artists feel like it was being done for them as well. It was an opportunity for them to help shape the lives of thousands of young people.

During the 1993 festival, I was with Hamp in his trailer listening to the Outstanding Young Artists concert. He said a prayer and put his hand on me, much like he was giving me a blessing, and asked that the festival would stay strong and have the Lord's blessing. Then he gave me a big hug and told me he really understood what I had in mind for the festival and that he was glad to be a part of it.

CHAPTER 2

A New Focus

"YOU LOOK TIRED."

This observation, offered by the University of Idaho provost's secretary in 1991, was accurate. I had been running the jazz festival for fourteen years, while continuing to be the head of the music education department, and it was taking a toll. There was a period I was teaching every music education class on campus—graduate and undergraduate—which was at least two people's full loads, at least six classes every semester. Plus, I was in charge of all the student teaching.

My first year at UI, I had forty-two student teachers out in the field, and every Tuesday and Thursday I was in my car by four in the morning, leaving Moscow, heading somewhere to see student teachers. One year I was teaching the vocal music classes, as well as all the instrumental classes. When I started doing the vocal classes, all of a sudden schools from around the state started asking me to do clinics with their vocal teams. So it was really more like three full teaching loads I had. And then, in 1977, I started running the jazz festival. Busy as I was, I always tried to be home at night, if I could, so I could spend some time with Elvon and our children. Then I'd go back and work some more. Adding to that, I was a bishop at my church, and that was a full-time job in itself. It was a tough time.

So, that day in 1991, I told the provost's secretary that if I didn't get some help, I couldn't physically keep going. Between the festival and my duties in the school of music, I was working seventeen or eighteen hours a day—five, sometimes six days a week. She must have said something to the provost, because about a week later he called me in for a meeting.

He told me the university was considering having the jazz festival report directly to the provost or the president. Then he offered me a choice: Did I want to remain as head of the music education department, or did I want to focus entirely on the jazz festival? I told him I felt that if I didn't do the jazz festival, it might not have the strength to keep growing. I told him I owed it to Hamp and to the jazz world to continue focusing on the festival.

You have to consider how I came into this. I had some playing experience. I certainly wasn't one of the jazz greats, but I had played a lot, I had that background. I had good skills on several instruments and an incredible love for jazz. I'd started the first jazz program in the public schools in Idaho, although hardly anyone on campus at that time knew that. I came to the festival with an incredible love for the music and for the artists who had made it happen, but also I came with a strong education in how to build programs and make changes. I also had a minor in motivational and deviant behavioral psychology. That's how I learned competition is a good motivator.

When I began focusing solely on running the festival, I was able to devote more time to fundraising. I worked hard to get the following year's performers booked by the middle of summer, and then I turned my attention to finding donors and sponsors.

Here's Hamp with my granddaughter, Katelyn, in the mid-1990s. She always called him Grandpa Hamp.

I found that competition worked as a motivator in that area as well. Banks, especially, seemed to enjoy vying with each other to support the festival. If one bank made a contribution, other banks invariably would match or exceed it so as to not be outdone. The office of the president of Zions Bank in Salt Lake City was decorated with posters from the Lionel Hampton Jazz Festival. By the mid-1990s, more than ninety corporations and individuals were supporting the festival with grants, scholarships, and donations of musical equipment.

Alaska Air provided dozens of tickets to artists to get them to the festival. In the 1990s, Ford provided eighty cars for volunteers to use to pick up performers, as well as a Lincoln Continental for Hamp's personal use.

CHAPTER 24

Memories of You ... and You and You and You ...

I'VE OFTEN BEEN ASKED TO NAME MY MOST MEMO-
rable festival, but I can't, really. If I looked at the schedule of any
given year of the festival, I could tell you of an experience that
was unbelievable.

Definitely one of the memorable festivals was 1984, the year
Sarah Vaughan performed. When a student volunteer arrived at
the Spokane airport to pick up Sarah in a regular four-door sedan,
she told him her contract stated she'd be picked up in a limou-
sine, and she refused to get in. Larry Clothier, her manager, who
became one of my closest friends, called a limo service in Spokane
and got her down to Moscow. Larry later became the manager of
Carmen McRae, Roy Hargrove, and Roberta Gambarini.

Benny Green and Hank Jones listening to me play
during a festival in the early 2000s.

Then, at about five in the afternoon on the Friday Sarah was
scheduled to perform, she said she wouldn't go onstage unless
she had her $10,000 check cashed. The banks were closed, and
people were just going nuts.

I said, "Go to the ticket office. They're selling tickets for
the ball games and stuff! There's got to be some cash on hand
somewhere around here!" Somehow we were able to get the cash
together, because Sarah was not going onstage until she had it in
her hand. Unfortunately, many performers—especially African
American women—have been cheated by promoters and others
over the years. Sarah, who began performing professionally in
1943, had probably experienced that herself, and she wasn't going
to take any chances.

In 1992, we had the great baritone sax player Gerry Mulligan.
We'd been working a long time to get him and he was finally able
to come. The Friday night concert got extended because Al Jarreau called Hamp up, and they started doing some stuff together.

Here's a shot of jazz trumpet legend Pete Candoli with members of my family in 2002.

It started getting later and later, and no one was leaving. It was after midnight, and we hadn't even brought on Gerry Mulligan. Hamp was still playing at one twenty in the morning, and the audience stayed right with it. I felt terrible about it, but there wasn't a thing you could do.

The next night, when Hamp's band started to play "Hamp's Boogie Woogie," Stan Getz was standing by me on the side of the

With David "Fathead" Newman and Clark Terry, in the mid-1990s.

Herb Ellis and Hank Jones enjoy a laugh with Grady Tate.

stage, and he started playing all these crazy riffs he used to play with Hamp many, many years before. I'd give anything to have a recording of that. It was just incredible. And then Hamp called him up, and he played with the band.

In the early years of the festival in Moscow, it didn't matter if it was the Ray Brown Trio, Stanley Turrentine, James Moody, Art Farmer, Clark Terry, Stan Getz, Gerry Mulligan—no matter who it was, they all wanted Hamp to come up and play a tune with them. The concerts would start at eight, and I'd think, "I'll have this done by eleven"—and then it would be one thirty in the morning. Hamp would come onstage and the audience wouldn't want him to leave.

One year, when Hank Jones and his brother, Elvin, were at the festival, Elvin put his arm around me, and said, "Doc, that stage up there is Hamp's living room. Would you like to have somebody come into your living room and tell you what to do?" And that ended it. We never talked about it again. If anybody asked about it, that's exactly what we told them: It was Hamp's living room. Some of those concerts went on longer than expected, but no one left without having their souls filled when Hamp was finished. The artists who performed with Hamp in Moscow gave so much. It was a new level of performance.

In 1983, Doc Severinsen, the great trumpet player from "The Tonight Show," came to the festival with his band. That year we also put a big band together with the original Four Freshmen. There were two or three guys living in Spokane who had played with the original Stan Kenton band, and I hired them to come down. Doc Severinsen was amazing, and did he ever put on a show. I got to visit with him later, and he was just a great, great guy.

I presented Dizzy Gillespie the Lionel Hampton Jazz Hall of Fame Award in 1988.

Another noteworthy year was 1988. While the 1988 festival turned out well in the end, various issues caused us to be so late lining up artists that year that a special insert had to be put in the program. Hamp got involved and asked Dizzy Gillespie to come to the festival. Dizzy agreed, and his presence was appreciated by all of us, since we'd been trying to get him since 1986. Other jazz greats who agreed to come on short notice that year included saxophonist Buddy Tate, and trombonist Al Grey. Notable groups that year included the Ray Brown Trio, with Brown on bass, Mickey Roker on drums, and Gene Harris on piano; and the Tommy Flanagan Trio, with Flanagan on piano, Kenny Washington on drums, and George Mraz on bass.

The Thursday night concert of the 1988 festival was called

Here I am with the wonderful pianist Mulgrew Miller.

"Great Women in Jazz," and included Betty Carter and her trio, as well as Ethel Ennis and Ernestine Anderson. Betty, Ethel, and Ernestine performed with the Ray Brown Trio with a tribute to women in jazz.

Another memorable year was 1995, when the documentary film *A Great Day in Harlem* premiered at the festival. The film, by Jean Bach, is about the making of the famous 1958 photo taken in Harlem by Art Kane, and featuring fifty-seven jazz artists. Marian McPartland, Art Farmer, Hank Jones, and Benny Golson—who are all in the photograph—signed a special copy of the poster and gave it to me as a gift. I will always cherish their dedication to jazz and their love for Hamp.

That was also the year of the great reunion of Hamp, Art Farmer and Benny Golson. Art and Benny had been in Hamp's band decades before, and when they went to Europe to play, Art fell in love with Germany, decided to stay there and didn't return with the band. He and Benny Golson had been roommates in the band, and did a lot of stuff together and recorded together,

Karriem Riggins, me, Ray Brown and Larry Fuller.

Hamp's love and enthusiasm for the festival was always evident by the ever-present smile on his face. This photo was taken in 1988.

Here I am with the great trombonist Al Grey during the final festival he attended in 2000. He died a month later.

but they had not seen each other for many years. I got in touch with Art in Germany and invited him to the festival. To see the look on Art's face when he walked out on that stage for the sound check, and there was Hamp. I saw a tear running down Art's cheek. Then to see Benny Golson walk out—to see this reunion take place! It was a highlight of my career.

Another great experience was with Al Grey at the 2000 festival. Dianne Reeves, who had first performed at the festival in 1982, when she was only twenty-five years old, was also at the festival that year. Now she was a Grammy Award-winning singer. As she prepared to go onstage, she said, "Doc, do you think Al Grey would come and play with me?" Hamp was sitting next to me, and he said, "Go ask him. He'd probably love it!"

Al was so tickled when he came out onstage with her. I didn't know it at the time, but he had played on one of her albums. She

Here was an all-star shot: In the back row is Russell Malone, Lewis Nash, Christian McBride, and Mulgrew Miller. In front are Al Grey, Bill Watrous, and Ian McDougal.

was so excited. That was the last festival Al attended. He died a month later.

As for the types of performers who come to the festival, there has always been a mixture. We bring in someone new and we get a new flavor when they perform with someone they never performed with before. Many artists tell me they think of the festival as their "second home." They feel like what happened there was a tribute to them, and so when they get there they're ready, as the boys in the band say, to "turn on the after-burners." They do an incredible push to try to make something special happen.

One year, I brought in Curtis Fuller, Al Grey, Ian McDougal, and Carl Fontana—four of the greatest trombone players in the world. We also had another trombone player—a young man who had not made up his mind whether he wanted to be a performer or a producer. He could have done either, because he had an incredible ear and was a brilliant musician. That was Delfeayo Marsalis, Wynton Marsalis's younger brother. When Delfeayo

Three of the greats: Benny Powell, Carl Fontana, and Al Grey.

got to the festival, those four trombone players said, "You're coming out onstage with us." Delfeayo did a couple of numbers with them, and when he walked offstage, he came over to me and put his arm around me. He was so clearly filled with joy. It was a very emotional experience for him. He said, "Doc, I just learned more in those two pieces than I learned in my whole life. I've made a decision. This is what I have to do."

I later saw Delfeayo in California playing with Elvin Jones—and what a treat that was, to see how he had developed into a great, great trombonist.

CHAPTER 25

Hamp's Statue

IN THE FALL OF 1995, JAMES HILL, A FRIEND OF MINE who owned the Toyota dealership in Moscow, introduced me to his wife Denali. Denali was an artist who had done work for Nike, among others, and she was interested in doing a full-size statue of Lionel Hampton. The process began when she took Hamp's measurements at his motel room during the 1996 festival. It was fun to see Hamp so excited to have a statue made of him.

The next step was to collect as many photographs of Hamp as possible, so Denali could envision him as a young man and at various stages of his career. She started working on a clay model, and I would go and look at it as it progressed. Sometimes I even brought various staff members along to get their perspectives. There definitely was improvement every time, but at that stage the work-in-progress still didn't seem to capture Hamp's true likeness. One day Denali called me and said she felt she was getting very close with the clay model. I went to see it, and she was right.

But although the likeness was close, something still wasn't right. She asked me, "What does it need to really look like Hamp?"

I asked for some time alone with the model, and I closed my eyes and pictured Hamp in my mind. When I opened my eyes and looked at the model I knew the problem: the face was much too full. I told Denali what I thought needed to be done, and it was like magic when she called me a few hours later and told me the model was finished. I looked at it and agreed. It was Hamp.

After that part of the project was done, I asked Denali how much it would cost to have the statue done in bronze at a foundry in Joseph, Oregon. She said it would be close to $40,000. I called my friend, Bob Kirby, who was retired as CEO of Westinghouse, and told him what I was trying to do. I had been introduced to Bob by Hamp, and he and Hamp were close friends. When I told this extraordinarily generous man that the project would cost $40,000, not only did he not hesitate to help honor his friend, but he threw in an extra $5,000 to have a small version of the statue made for me. Bob later gave $250,000 to the Lionel Hampton School of Music for scholarships.

Hamp passed away in 2002, and in 2003, the first year of the festival without him, I saw that statue on the stage, and it filled my heart with emotion. I felt like Hamp was still there with me, saying, "Let's go, Doc. We've got it together, let's keep going."

That year we had a special celebration of Lionel Hampton's life and music, and more than seventy-five artists came to Idaho in the middle of February for the four-day event. That's the kind of event Hamp's vision inspired.

After Hamp's passing, we didn't slow down. The kids kept coming, and the quality of the artists was the finest in the world. I tried to have a lot of variety. We'd have the house quartet do three tunes, and then another group do a few tunes. We'd have two sax players come out. They'd do a tune together and then do tunes with one or the other of them taking the lead. They'd just work it out and make it happen. I had to be careful that you didn't have a solo by everybody in the rhythm section. That happened a couple of times, and the concerts didn't end until two in the morning.

But we worked that out. We made a poster of me dressed in a doctor's uniform and saying, "Doc says take two choruses, and don't call me in the morning." The artists really respected that. We never had anyone taking more than two choruses. Hamp told me one time a musician in his band wanted to do a few choruses, and he took thirty-six before he stopped. That was the last time he played with Hamp.

CHAPTER 26

Clint Eastwood Makes Our Day

I KNEW CLINT EASTWOOD WAS A TRUE JAZZ LOVER. I'D been trying to get him to the festival for years, but it never worked out with his schedule. Then in 1991, Hamp was playing a concert in Carmel, California, where Clint Eastwood was mayor. They knew each other, and Hamp asked Clint to come to the festival the following year. I think it was the very next morning that I got a call from Clint's manager telling me Clint would come to the festival. I called Hamp and told him, and he said, "Put his name in big letters at the top of the poster."

I told Clint's manager what Hamp had in mind for the poster, and she said she'd talk to Clint. She called me back and told me Clint knew what the festival was about, that it was about Hamp touching the lives of young people. She said Clint wanted his name at the very bottom of the poster in the smallest letters you could use: "Clint Eastwood, special guest of Lionel Hampton."

Hollywood legend and jazz lover Clint Eastwood was awarded the Lionel Hampton Jazz Hall of Fame Award at the 1992 festival in Moscow.

Hamp really didn't want to do that, but I told him I was afraid that if we didn't do as Clint asked, he might not show up. As I recall, Clint flew to the festival in his own plane. The jazz festival volunteer who picked him up at the airport said she got so nervous she almost forgot where she was supposed to take him.

When word got out that Clint Eastwood was coming to the festival, practically every police officer, sheriff's deputy, fire-fighter, and state trooper from around the region wanted to have a photo taken with him. I said I would ask him, because I didn't know how he would feel about it. He said, "You find a place, and we'll do it. There's nothing more important to me than doing this for the people who keep us safe."

All these people had their pictures taken with Clint and got copies of the photos later. We had a special room set up at the Best Western motel where the artists from the festival could hang out and ticket-holders could go and mingle with the artists. That year, we had photos of the artists who had performed at the festival over the years displayed on the walls of the room. I went out there and found Clint walking around the room looking at the photos.

He said, "Doc, they weren't lying to me. I've never seen anything like this in my life. I can hardly believe this is taking place." I enjoyed seeing how Clint reacted to people. Sometimes you get a big star, and everything has to be written out ahead of time, and you wouldn't dare ask them to do something that wasn't in the contract. That was something I dealt with when Wynton Marsalis came to the festival. His manager said, "No clinics for Wynton." But when Wynton got to the airport, he called me and said, "That guy doesn't know what he's talking about. That's why I'm here."

Clint was so good with people. Even all the officers who were working at the concerts got a chance to have their photo taken with him. Someone who's willing to do something special for other people like that will never be forgotten. That's going to live on for who knows how many generations, in the lives of those people who had their picture taken with Clint Eastwood.

When Clint came to Moscow, we gave him the Lionel Hampton Jazz Festival Hall of Fame Award. It was a plaque with Hamp's signature engraved on it, and when Clint saw it, he was really touched. He had tears in his eyes. We gave it to him because of his love of jazz. Clint said listening to and playing jazz was invaluable to his career as an actor and director because he learned how to improvise and try different things in his movies. It was neat to be able to see him reach people. He talked about some of his movies. He talked about jazz in his own life and what a difference it had made to him. He encouraged the thousands of kids who were listening to keep doing what they were doing and not give up. It meant so much to Hamp to have Clint there.

CHAPTER 27

Jazz in the Schools

IN THE MID-1990S, WE STARTED THINKING OF THINGS we could do to enhance the festival. One of the women who helped me book performers said, "When I talk to them, why don't I ask them to come a day early, and we'll start a Jazz in the Schools program?" Every artist she asked came a day early, and we started the program, which involved artists visiting public schools in the region to perform for the students and talk about jazz.

That first year we had people playing all over the place. When I called Hamp and told him what was happening, he said, "I want to be involved in this."

I brought him down to Lapwai, a small town on the Nez Perce reservation about forty miles south of Moscow, to do a clinic for the Native American kids. He ended up having an incredible relationship with these students, and every year they played traditional Native American music for him, and he would play for them. The kids would dance and just really get into it. One year

I gave an almost life-size photograph of Hamp to the school. I don't know if it's still there, but it was hanging above the water fountain in the school, where all the students could see it.

One year, the students gave Hamp an eagle feather, the most valuable gift a Native American can give. In fact, they even gave Hamp an Indian name: Flying Eagle. Every once in a while I'd call him and ask, "How's Flying Eagle doing today?" and he'd say, "Man, I'm flying higher than I have in a long time, now that you've called, Doc."

Hamp respected what those Native American students had done for him, and he loved to talk about how much it meant to him that the Nez Perce made him feel he was part of their culture and lives. That was the way Hamp liked to do it with everybody. He did that with my entire family. He just wanted us to feel like we were a part of his life. He certainly was a part of ours.

When we started the Jazz in the Schools program, we had one person helping me with the scheduling, but after two or three years, the program got so big that we had to have someone working full-time on it. It was becoming too big of a load for me. I loved doing it, because I knew most of the directors, but with everything else I was doing, it was too much. We hired a woman to help with it, and she was incredible. She lined up everything. The wonderful thing was the artists didn't mind where they went. Whether it was Moscow, Lewiston, Coeur d'Alene, Spokane, or any small town in between. Some artists even went to Sun Valley, Idaho Falls, Rexburg, and Montpelier. When I brought the artists to Montpelier, there would literally be a couple thousand people attending the performance at a Mormon tabernacle. I took several different groups to Montpelier over the years, and every year, in the front row, would be thirty or forty older people who had graduated from the University of Idaho. The experience brought tears of joy to their eyes.

At one point we had about 15,000 students involved in the Jazz in the Schools program. Journalists loved going to the Jazz in the Schools clinics, especially at Lapwai. Sometimes we had practically a busload of journalists going to the programs. Later, the National Endowment for the Arts found out about it and started a program to help bring live music to schools around the country. When we hear music live, there is a communication we can't get from listening to a recording.

CHAPTER 28

Dewaylon McCoy

I'M AWARE NOT EVERY CHILD HAS HAD THE SUPPORT and encouragement in their musical pursuits that I received, but in my years with the Lionel Hampton Jazz Festival, I witnessed countless times when the power of music transformed the lives of young people.

One was in 1994, when we got a phone call from Dallas, Texas. There was a young African American boy there named Dewaylon McCoy who wanted to come and play at the festival, but he didn't have a penny to his name. He wanted to play vibes, but the only thing he had that was anything like a vibraphone was an old set of tone bells his school had given him. He had fixed it so it kind of looked like a set of vibes, and he was teaching himself how to play on these little tone bells. I called Hamp and told him about it, and he said, "We need to get him here."

The following year, 1995, we provided a scholarship so Dewaylon could attend the festival. He was eleven years old, and

Dewaylon McCoy of Dallas, Texas, hugs Lionel Hampton
after performing with him at Lionel Hampton Jazz Festival
in 1995. Dewaylon returned to the festival in 1996.

he brought his grandmother with him. He was a wonderful young man. We got him here—got him rehearsing and playing tunes with Lionel Hampton. He just idolized Hamp.

CBS News found out about Dewaylon and featured him in a story they did on the festival that year. The story was seen all over the country. Billy Taylor interviewed Dewaylon in Dallas, and then interviewed Hamp.

Shortly after the story aired, I got a phone call from a man in California named Jerry King, who had seen it. He said he had a Musser vibraphone he hadn't played for years, and he wanted to give it to Dewaylon. It was unbelievable. The instrument was worth thousands of dollars. He shipped it to my office at the university, and later we shipped it to Dewaylon's home in Dallas. I called the boy's home later and was told he cried when he received the vibes. But that's only part of the story.

Jonathan Eig, who was then with the *Dallas Morning News,* and later with the *Wall Street Journal,* covered the festival that year and had written several stories. He called me after the festival and said he wanted to do something more to help Dewaylon. He told me a music teacher in Dallas, who was one of the best vibes teachers in the area, said if someone could get Dewaylon there, he would give him lessons for free. Then Jonathan told me he would drive Dewaylon to the lessons himself.

Dewaylon came to the festival the following year—but then we lost track of him. We have no idea what happened. When we tried to find him, there was no answer at the phone numbers we had for him. But I remember so well his grandmother being at the festival with him and how proud she was of that little boy as he stood there with Lionel Hampton and played a tune with him on stage. It must have been the dream of a lifetime for that young boy.

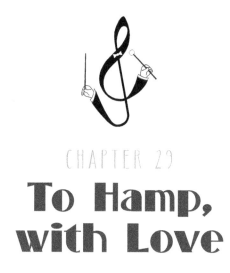

CHAPTER 29

To Hamp,
with Love

HAMP WAS CHANGING THE LIVES OF YOUNG MUSI-
cians long before he ever came to the jazz festival in Moscow. In
1999, as a belated gift for Hamp's ninetieth birthday, I recorded
interviews with more than a dozen musicians who'd had a relationship with Hamp over the years. I put them on a CD called *To
Hamp, with Love*.

Bassist Christian Fabian was thirteen when he first saw
Hamp's big band perform in his hometown in Germany. He said
he had just recently begun to play the bass, but that he wasn't
particularly inspired to perform or even practice. Hamp's concert
changed all that. At the end of the show, the band played "When
the Saints Go Marching In," and walked through the audience.

"I was really impressed," Christian said. "I thought, *Look at
those guys! They have so much fun playing music.*"

This photo of me, Benny Powell, and Al Grey is from the 1990s.

Hamp didn't just love music. He loved the men and women who made it come alive—who shared the language of music, the language of the soul. He always had time to support and encourage his fellow musicians.

Grammy Award-winning producer and musician Quincy Jones was just fifteen when he met Hamp. It was 1948, and the band was playing the Palomar Theatre in Seattle. Quincy was ready to join the band right then, but Hamp told him he needed to finish school first. When he did, Hamp brought him into the band, and as with so many other musicians Hamp mentored, Quincy's life was never the same.

"I'll never forget ... we were playing the Band Box at Birdland and we wore Tyrolean hats and the purple jackets and Bermuda shorts. We were marching upstairs, and we were playing drum-sticks all over the awning, and there was Thelonious Monk, Bud Powell, Bird, Miles, Dizzy, and everybody else next door. I remember when Bird came in to sit in with us at Birdland before we went to Europe."

Pianist Bill Charlap, who first performed at the Lionel Hampton Jazz Festival in 1999, was a freshman in high school when he first heard Hamp—on a recording called "Hallelujah," which Hamp did with Art Tatum. He said he had never heard anything like it. Bill met Hamp when they were both performing at a jazz concert in the late 1990s.

"After I walked offstage, he asked me himself if I would be part of the festival," Bill said. "That was a thrill I can't express."

Trombonist Al Grey met Hamp in 1947 and joined his band shortly thereafter. In the interview I did with him for Hamp's

Here I am with the trumpeters Claudio Roditi and Joe Giorgianni.

birthday CD, Al recalled how Hamp taught him how to clap his hands for rhythm and how to take a bow.

"Lionel took an interest in me, and he said, 'Hey, Gates, you do it this way.' And I've seen him do this for so many artists." (The term "Gates" originated in the 1920s, and refers to a jazz musician's ability to "swing like a gate.")

Al recalled a performance with Hamp at the Hollywood Bowl around 1980, when the band followed Grover Washington Jr., whose song "Just the Two of Us" was a big hit at the time. "Of course, when you have a hit on the market, everyone is for that hit," Al said. "And we had to follow that."

As the double-sided stage slowly spun around to face the audience, Hamp and his bandmates could see people leaving the auditorium. "Then, all of a sudden, Lionel Hampton walked down to the edge of the stage and just started clapping his hands to a beat. We went into it, and the next thing I know everyone was turning around and coming back to their seats. Everyone came back into the Bowl, all around the stage, and when Lionel Hampton finished, they were just screaming, 'More, more, more!'"

Hamp always had a way with audiences. He just wanted to bring his message of music across, and he was good at it. He spent his life doing it. He knew that if that meant getting up and dancing, or whatever he needed to do, he was going to do it, because he wanted to get the attention of everyone in the room. That was the amazing thing about Hamp. He could bring a group of people together and help them learn a greater love of the music than they'd ever had before.

The great Brazilian-born trumpet player Claudio Roditi talked about how impressed he was with Hamp's knowledge of various jazz styles. Claudio was performing, along with Arturo Sandoval, at the festival in Moscow one year, and one of the tunes they intended to play was "Speak Low," a tune that has chord changes that are similar to bebop. He said he was surprised when Hamp announced he wanted to play the tune with Claudio's group.

"Of course, everybody knows he is coming more from the Swing Era, and one forgets that he lived through the whole bebop history. I cannot tell you how surprised I was to see the fluidity that Hamp had blowing over the chord changes of 'Speak Low.' It sounded like he was born in that era and was absolutely familiar with that type of playing."

At the 1998 festival—the year Hamp turned ninety—Claudio performed a tune he'd written for the occasion called "A Song for Hamp." The tune was in a Brazilian samba style for which Claudio was well-known. Nonetheless, it was "a kind of music that is not so much a part of Lionel Hampton's tradition," he said.

"At rehearsal [...] while we were running through the tune [...] I saw Hamp was sitting on the side of the stage. I'm wondering, *Gee, is this something that he is going to like? Is he into this kind of music?*" The band rehearsed the tune a little, and then did a complete rundown of it.

Claudio continued: "Hamp calls everybody 'Gates,' as we all know, and he calls me, and says, 'Hey, Gates, come over here.' He looks at me and says, 'Can you get me a copy of that tune?' That made me feel so good, because it was proof he enjoyed the song. That made me feel very, very good."

I had a similar experience with Hamp in 1990, when I was working on a piece called "Gray is Never Really Blue." While we were setting up the festival, someone asked me to check out the sound on the house piano. I'm sure they thought I would just hit a few notes, but I started playing my new tune. I didn't know Hamp was around, but when he heard me playing, he walked up to the stage.

"Doc, why didn't you tell me?"

"Tell you what?"

"That's a nice piece. Where did you get it?"

"Well, I wrote it."

"You composed that? I want you to play that with my band! Don't tell anybody. We'll say we have a surprise guest artist and you're going to come out and play that tune on your tenor saxophone. I'll have it arranged."

I still have that arrangement.

On *To Hamp, with Love,* saxophonist and vocalist Lance Bryant talked about the evening he spent with Hamp, when he began to learn "how the old masters created this music." He got the chance to see Lionel practice and work out a tune.

"We were working on a tune that he had me do the arrangement for. We were going to record it soon, and so we both sat at the piano in his apartment. While I played the chords, chorus after chorus, he would solo over the chord changes. There was this one particular line he kept doing, and every time we got to a particular part in the chord progression, he would play this line over and over. He would develop it; he would do a little variation of it on every chorus. As I sat there listening to him, I got the feeling this is how the cat always developed what he did. It was a nice little revelation for me."

Lance said that when he asked Hamp about what he and his musicians had done years ago, Hamp didn't have much to say. Instead, Hamp wanted to talk about what Lance and his band were doing and what they were planning to do. Hamp was a "very forward-thinking, contemporary guy," Lance said. He didn't seem to want to talk much about history. That is, Lance said, "unless you wanted to talk about Louis Armstrong."

Bassist David Friesen heard stories about Hamp from the pianist and vibes player Elmer Gill, when Friesen and Gill worked together in the mid-1960s. Gill, who had worked in Hamp's band in the early 1950s, also had stories about other members of Hamp's band during the period, including Charlie Parker, Gigi Gryce, Wes Montgomery, and many others.

"Obviously, from what Elmer told me, Lionel made a substantial positive impact on so many musicians' lives," David told me.

David first saw Hamp perform at the Newport Jazz Festival in the late 1970s, where David was performing as a member of the Ted Curson Sextet.

"It seemed to me at the time, while watching and listening to his band, here was a man that had been truly blessed, not only with the gift of playing music, but also the ability to communicate his love for the music to so many people with so many different tastes. His ability to sidestep the difference of opinions and make his way into the hearts of so many was very obvious."

David was performing at the 1996 Lionel Hampton Jazz Festival with pianist Oliver Jones and drummer Elvin Jones, when

The wonderful vocalist Dee Daniels has performed at the festival nineteen times, including many times during my years as executive director. I believe this photo was taken in the early 1990s.

Hamp walked onstage in the middle of their concert and started playing along with them on vibes.

"It kind of takes all the pretentiousness out," David said. "It brings things down to ground zero: the love of music."

David got to talk to Hamp backstage after the performance, and that night, Hamp was happy to talk about the old days.

"I asked about Elmer Gill, and as though it was just yesterday, he started to relate stories about Elmer and the band in the fifties, and all these great experiences, and I just listened."

Vocalist Dee Daniels also received an unannounced visit from Hamp onstage during her performance at the 1992 jazz festival in Moscow. It was the first time she met Hamp.

"I remember sitting at the piano, on the second song of my set, and I was just singing away some bluesy version of a gospel tune, and I had my eyes closed. I was deep in concentration. Just before I was about to take a solo chorus, I just happened to open my eyes, and there was Lionel standing about five feet away from me, in his typical Lionel stance—arms outstretched, mallets in each hand, with a big grin on his face—and I was so surprised. The next thing I knew, he was over at his vibes, and he took the solo. For the briefest moment, I realized that I was onstage with this living legend, Mr. Lionel Hampton. And not only that [...] I was actually accompanying him on piano."

The legendary bassist Milt Hinton, who died in 2000 at age ninety, first met Hamp in 1930, when Hamp picked up Milt's trio at the Los Angeles railroad station and took them to their hotel on Central Avenue. In 1936, while performing with Cab Calloway at the Cotton Club, Milt saw Hamp perform with the Benny Goodman Quartet at the Pennsylvania Hotel.

On *To Hamp, with Love*, Milt related a story about playing in Hamp's band at a concert on the Potomac River in Washington, DC, in the 1950s. Louis Armstrong's All-Stars opened the show. Not surprisingly, following Louis Armstrong was no easy feat, and the band that followed Louis Armstrong (Milt couldn't recall the name of the band) had a hard time getting the crowd going again. That is, until the band played Hamp's hit tune "Flying Home," and "the audience went wild," Milt said.

"When Lionel came on stage with his band and heard [the previous band] had already played 'Flying Home,' he had a trick up his sleeve. When we played 'Splash,' we all jumped in the river! The audience was screaming and cheering and stomping. Hamp had done it again."

Always the showman, Hamp closed his concerts with "Flying Home" for years, including many performances at the jazz festival in Moscow. Saxophonist James Moody, who performed at the Lionel Hampton Jazz Festival several times, recalled dropping by New York's Paramount Theatre to catch Hamp's show.

"I had my horn with me, and you know Hamp, he says, 'Come on, Gates, come on out and play with us on this last number.'" The band started to play "Flying Home," and at the end of the tune, Hamp motioned for Moody to take the solo.

"They didn't tell me that at the end of 'Flying Home,' an explosion would go off and smoke would fill the stage. So you can imagine what happened while I was playing! I looked at Hamp, and he says, 'Yeah, Gates! Go, go, go, go!'"

Years later, when Moody was invited by Hamp to join the group the Golden Men of Jazz, he witnessed Hamp's unbounded energy and creativity once again.

"I really enjoyed that," he recalled. "There was Harry 'Sweets' Edison, Clark Terry, Al Grey, Ingrid Jensen, Benny Golson, Panama Francis, Jimmy Woode, Junior Mance, of course, Hamp, and myself. We did the Blue Note in New York, and it was packed every night. If you really wanted to see Hamp come alive, just outdo himself, you let him come up onstage, and the people start clapping, and boy, he would outdo himself—every night. It was a wonderful experience to get to play with Lionel Hampton and just watch him in action."

Pianist Kuni Mikami, who moved to New York from Japan

in 1975, first worked with Hamp in 1991, on a European tour. Kuni had been working as a freelance pianist in New York City, but when Hamp took him to Europe, he said it opened up a whole new world to him and broadened his vision of what being jazz performer could mean. After that tour, Kuni performed with Hamp all over the world. They performed "The Star-Spangled Banner" at an Atlanta Braves baseball game, and they played for Texas governor George W. Bush. But Kuni said the thing that amazed him most about performing with Hamp was watching him do his solos.

"When he plays solos—and he'll be playing this tune every night—his solo sounds fresh, every night. Whether it's 'How High the Moon,' or any kind of tune he plays a million times, I never get bored. I'm always listening, enjoying his solo. There's some secret there—I don't know what—but I'd like to find out the secret of his solo."

I had the same feeling about Hamp's solos. It blew my mind to hear rehearsal after rehearsal, concert after concert, at the festival in Moscow and other places, and to realize that Hamp never played a solo the same way. It was always something different. He just had that ability.

Hamp lived for sharing music, and his love of music allowed him to overcome circumstances that probably would have done in a lesser man. The drummer Wally Gator Watson related a story of playing with Hamp's big band on a twenty-seven-day, twenty-four-city European tour in the mid-1990s.

"[It was] a very grueling schedule by any standards, and we had to do the whole tour by bus, due to a general strike in Europe that didn't allow us to fly. We had a lot of eleven- and twelve-hour bus rides."

Hamp, who was in his late eighties at the time, held up "amazingly well," Wally said. "A lot of us guys were tired of riding the bus, but Hamp, being the true champ that he is, was hanging right on in there."

Hamp had a bed on the bus, and as the band was on the way to Paris, the bus went around a curve, and Hamp rolled out of bed. "We all woke up to a loud thump when Lionel hit the floor. Lionel looked up and said, 'Whoa, Gates! That was quite a drop!'"

Hamp seemed to be doing okay, but three or four songs into the Paris concert, it became obvious he was not. "He was having a major stroke right there onstage in front of everybody's eyes," Wally recalled. "They rushed him off to the hospital, and I've got to say that I really kind of thought that was the end for Lionel."

A week later, Wally got a call from Mount Sinai Hospital and was asked if he would assist with giving Lionel some therapy on drums. "This was quite a challenge for me. I'm not a physical therapist or anything," Wally said.

"But I developed some drum exercises to try and strengthen his left side, where he was affected the most. I brought some electronic drums to the hospital, got Hamp up and got him on the drums, put the headphones on him and started putting him through the paces." After fifteen minutes, Hamp was exhausted, and the session stopped. Wally was doubtful the therapy would work. Hamp went to bed, and Wally went home, leaving the drum set with Hamp.

Wally got a surprise when he returned to the hospital the next day. A nurse told him Hamp had gotten up several times during the night and done the drum exercises by himself. By the next day, Hamp was able to do a half-hour session on the drums, and he continued to progress rapidly.

"Within three months, Hamp was back to playing. We were playing the Kool Jazz Festival in New York, and it was really an honor to be a part of that and see the true essence of the inner man, a true champion, a man who did not give up on himself, did not give up on his music, and did not give up on his people."

CHAPTER 30

Pieces of Jazz History

THE UNIVERSITY OF IDAHO'S INTERNATIONAL JAZZ Collections started with some musical scores and other materials Hamp donated shortly after the school of music was renamed. Later, the school received the collections of Leonard Feather, Al Grey, Pete and Conte Candoli, Joe Williams, Stan Kenton, Dizzy Gillespie, Ray Brown, Ella Fitzgerald, Buddy Tate, Doc Cheatham, and others. The university also received copies of materials in Gerry Mulligan's collection—the original collection had been donated to the National Archives.

When Al Grey died in Arizona, his wife called me literally from Al's hospital room. She said, "The last thing we were talking about is you, Doc. Al told me, 'I want my collection where Doc is.'"

Many of Ella Fitzgerald's things had already been sold because they were bringing a lot of money. I called someone with Ella's estate and told him about the jazz festival and what we were doing with the International Jazz Collections project, and asked if we could have some of Ella's collection for the University of Idaho.

He said, "I'll set aside one of her black performance dresses, a pair of shoes, her eyeglasses, and one of her hats for you."

The collection later grew to include fifty-two of Ella's items, including other hats, gowns, jewelry, records, photographs, a wig, credit cards, programs from Norman Granz's Jazz at the Philharmonic, and a lead vocal arrangement for "Begin the Beguine."

The collection includes several instruments, but there also are a lot of musical scores. Jazz musicians had hundreds of scores they used when they were playing. The University of Idaho library has taken good care of the jazz collection. There have been some really good people over the years who have genuinely cared about it and want to make it available for people to see. If you love jazz, there's no way you can stand in front of Al Grey's hat, and the trombone he played, and not have it touch your heart in some way.

I had spoken to Leonard Feather on the telephone in September 1994, when he was in the hospital, just to try to lift his spirits a little bit, to tell him how much we needed him, how important he was to the jazz world.

After Leonard passed, I attended his memorial service in Los Angeles, and I brought some photographs of him that were taken backstage at the jazz festival. I had three or four of them printed, and one I had enlarged and put in a beautiful frame to give to Mrs. Feather. I was sitting next to her during the service, and when it was over I gave her the photograph. She broke down for a moment, and then said, "I don't know if I've ever had anything that means as much as this picture."

Later, we discussed the idea of housing the Leonard Feather collection at the University of Idaho. She told me that was where Leonard wanted his collection to go. The collection includes all his books and recordings, his photographs of artists, and even tape recordings of the Blindfold Tests, where he tested the jazz knowledge of well-known jazz artists. They've got them all digitized now. You can go to the University of Idaho library, where the jazz collections are housed, and listen to them. The university is working to make the third floor of the library the home for the entire collection.

In the summer of 2016, I learned from one of Virginia Wicks's daughters (Virginia was the publicity director of the Lionel Hampton Jazz Festival from 1994 to 2006) that Virginia's entire collection—including correspondence with Ella Fitzgerald and other jazz stars, photographs of jazz artists, and other items— would be donated to the International Jazz Collections.

Sometimes it seems like people think someone just snapped their fingers and these things happened. But these things happened because I asked, and because I had wonderful relationships with these artists' families.

Around 1997, we started talking about the idea of a Lionel Hampton Center. The plan included a performing arts center, offices for the jazz festival, and an addition to the school of music—including remodeling the auditorium and putting in offices so the music faculty would be in the same building. We had a grant from Congress to hire experts to get it started, and it was on its way. We went to Cincinnati, Boston, Seattle, Portland and other cities to check out various performing arts facilities.

The project was going to be announced in 2000, and Hamp wanted it to be called the Hampton-Skinner Center because he didn't want it to be forgotten after he was gone. He thought that with my name attached to it, it would be more secure, because of my long affiliation with the university and the school of music.

Then we got a new president at the university. He was only there for a year, but he axed the Lionel Hampton Center. President George H.W. Bush himself, who, as I've said, was a great friend of Hamp's, was willing to help raise the money for the project. Then the next university president came in, and he could have revived it, but he seemed to be afraid to even talk to people. So the Lionel Hampton Center was out. I doubt anyone is going to bring it back now. It's sad that it was lost over someone's lack of vision and lack of concern for the arts. University officials never even gathered anyone together to discuss it. It wasn't right. I think they had the right people on board to be able to raise the money needed to make the Lionel Hampton Center a reality.

CHAPTER 31

Hamp's Jazz Festival: A Great Place to Start

I WAS AT A FESTIVAL BOARD MEETING IN 2007, ALONG with John Clayton and Jeff Hamilton. Just as we were preparing to get some lunch, Jeff got a call on his cell phone. He walked over to me and said, "I have someone who really wants to talk to you, Doc. It's Diana Krall."

I had first heard about Diana soon after she had made a recording with Ray Brown, one of her mentors. Ray called me in the summer of 1995 and told me there was this delightful and charming young lady who had incredible piano chops and also sang very well. He said he'd already mailed me a copy of her CD, and told me she was being represented by Mary Ann Topper in New York, someone I knew very well.

Lionel "Freddy" Cole during a festival in the late-1990s.

When the CD arrived, I listened to it carefully, and I was excited to hear the quality of her playing and singing. I immediately called Hamp and played it for him over the phone, and he also was impressed. Then I called Mary Ann, who told me Diana would really like to meet Hamp. I called Hamp, and he said, "Send her over tonight." Diana went over to Hamp's apartment and brought him a dozen roses and really impressed him. Hamp called me and told me she had played the piano like something he had rarely heard. I knew when Hamp said this that it was very good. He loved Diana so much, and he was so proud of her.

The day after I heard from Hamp, I called Diana's manager and found out Diana was performing in Victoria, British Columbia, with guitarist Russell Malone, pianist Benny Green, and bassist Ben Wolfe. So Elvon and I decided to go hear her.

We had seats near the back of this incredible auditorium, and when Diana started to play, we discovered we were sitting right next to her parents. What a neat experience it was to meet them. The love they showed for their daughter was like a magical treat for anyone. She was certainly the apple of their eyes. Diana did the Nat "King" Cole tribute, and it was truly a splendid concert.

When I got back to Moscow, I immediately signed Diana for the 1996 festival, where she performed with the Ray Brown Trio. Ray was very proud of her, and as the audience warmed to Diana's style and ability, we saw something special taking place.

That's how it is at the festival. It's a training field. Grammy Award-winning singer Dianne Reeves, who has performed at the festival numerous times—most recently in 2015—performed at the festival in 1983. I believe she has performed at the festival nearly a dozen times over the years. The New York Voices, as well as vocalist Jane Monheit performed at the Lionel Hampton Jazz Festival very early in their careers.

Vocalist Jane Monheit performed at the festival several times and was always a big hit with fans.

This was a young man from San Diego whose nickname was Snooki Thomas. He graduated from the Berklee College of Music.

Pianist Eldar Djangirov performed twice at the festival when he was teenager.

It's amazing the difference the festival made for somebody like Lionel "Freddy" Cole. I got the feeling Freddy's whole life as a performer changed after the first time he played at the festival—and he wasn't a young man at that point either. The people who saw him perform realized he was a very special talent. Later, he even played and recorded with the Dizzy Gillespie Big Band.

I'll always remember an incredible young pianist named Eldar Djangirov, whose family moved to the US from Kyrgyzstan when he was ten. He performed at the Lionel Hampton Jazz Festival twice as a young teenager. Now he is a major recording artist and is known all over the world. It's been amazing to see how the festival keeps touching lives.

CHAPTER 32

Another First: National Medal of Arts

I RETIRED AS EXECUTIVE DIRECTOR OF THE LIONEL Hampton Jazz Festival in 2007, after thirty-one years. John Clayton, who had been performing at the festival for ten years, was named the festival's Artistic Director, a position he held until 2016.

I was honored by the University of Idaho at the 2007 festival for my three decades of service to the festival. My work was honored again that same year, when the festival received the National Medal of Arts, the most prestigious arts award in the country, from President George W. Bush. It was the first time a music festival of any kind had received the award.

The way it happened was this: in late October, 2007, I got a call from the jazz festival office, telling me I needed to call

University of Idaho president Tim White right away. His secretary got him on the phone, and he got right to the point.

"Doc, something very important has happened. You and I have been invited to go to Washington, DC, to receive the National Medal of Arts award from President Bush." He said there would be some other people there, but that he wanted me to represent the university with him on the stage. He told me, "You did all the work to get the festival where it is."

The ceremony was in mid-November, and the university arranged the flight and the hotel and took care of everything. I was particularly excited because my old friend, Larry Grimes, was going to be there.

I remember it was raining

The Lionel Hampton Jazz Festival was awarded the National Medal of Arts in 2007, making it the first and only music festival of any kind to receive the award.

hard when we were admitted to the White House, where the ceremony was to take place. The audience stood as President George W. Bush and First Lady Laura Bush entered the room, and soon the ceremony was under way.

A number of awards were presented, and then it was time for the University of Idaho to be honored for the Lionel Hampton Jazz Festival. I had risen from my seat to head toward the stage when Tim turned to me and said, "Oh, you're not going up, Doc.

John Clayton's going to be with me on the stage." So I just sat there and watched.

The funny thing was, I was sitting near some of my friends who were members of the National Endowment for the Arts. I had served on several committees for the organization, and I knew a lot of people. One of them said, "Doc, what the hell is going here? You're supposed to be up there getting that award."

There really wasn't anything I could do about it, but I felt like there was going to be some backlash against the university, and there certainly was. President White never did tell me why he made that decision. To this day, I don't know why. I have friends who are still upset about it. I've tried to let it go, but it never should have happened like that. It was too bad, too, because I think it would have meant a lot more to the jazz festival if John and I had both been up on the stage with President White.

My granddaughter, Avarie, won an award for her vocal performance at the 2007 festival.

Many school music directors, colleagues, and friends were upset about what happened. Some of them were quite angry, in fact. You just have to let it go, because you can't let something like that eat you alive. But I thought it was in bad taste, and it was difficult to understand. After all, neither Tim White nor John Clayton had done *anything* for the festival. To me, the most important thing they had *not* done was acknowledge Virginia Wicks for all she had done for the festival.

The night before the awards ceremony, at a meeting with members of the NEA and those who would be receiving awards, I tried to make clear how important Virginia was to the festival's growth and success. When the president of the NEA asked me to talk about the festival, he said, "There was a big change that happened there. What was it?"

I told him it was because of Virginia Wicks, who started getting the word out about the festival to media all over the world. She was the festival's publicist from 1994 to 2006, and what she did for the festival was amazing. The festival owes a great deal to her. She really knew the business side of publicity, and a lot of good came to the festival because of her. In 1995, for example, journalists from Australia, Japan, France, Germany, Russia, Great Britain, New York, Chicago, Dallas, Los Angeles, San Francisco, Washington, DC, and numerous other cities came to cover the festival.

CHAPTER 33

Saying Goodbye to Hamp

HAMP ATTENDED EVERY FESTIVAL FROM 1984 TO 2002. His brief performance in 2002 was to be the final one of his long and illustrious career, and he died on August 31, 2002. What had been a small festival in 1984 when Hamp first got involved, was now known around the world, featured the best jazz artists in the business, and attracted thousands of students and jazz lovers year after year. The year 2002 was a tough one for me. In addition to Hamp's passing, my mother died on May 22, and Ray Brown died on July 3.

Hamp and I talked just about every day, and his spirit was strong even two days before he died. The day before he died, I called to see how he was doing, and his aide told me they were about to take him the hospital. When Hamp realized I was on the phone, he got on the line and said, "Doc, no matter what happens, just know I love you, and be ready to carry the torch."

I heard about Hamp's passing within minutes. I had known for several days that he was failing, but that didn't ease the pain in my heart. I spent most of the next ninety-six hours on the telephone talking with friends and journalists—sometimes crying, sometimes laughing, and always remembering the love Hamp gave me.

I vowed to carry on his desire to have that same love felt by all the students and artists who attended the festival. Even though I was sad, I realized that what Hamp had created with the festival was going to go on.

Elvon and I flew to New York City for Hamp's funeral, where I was to be a pallbearer. I was deeply touched by the musical tributes offered by the members of Hamp's big band. There was the touching hymn played by Hank Jones, and music poured forth from Illinois Jacquet, Jon Faddis, Wynton Marsalis, and Carrie Smith. Hamp's influence and inspiration were clear as these great musicians offered their talent and love.

Former president George H.W. Bush let the tears of joy,

Elvon, Hamp, myself and Hamp's valet at a concert in the 1990s.

love, and loss slide down his cheeks as he recounted his lifetime of memories. Hamp's attorney, Tim Francis, told about Hamp holding a benefit concert in London in 1956 to raise money for the legal defense of a group of South African dissidents who were on death row. One of those dissidents was Nelson Mandela.

University of Idaho President Bob Hoover spoke of Hamp's love of education and his support of many fine programs at the university, including the Lionel Hampton Jazz Festival, the Lionel Hampton School of Music, and the International Jazz Collections.

The procession began at the famed Cotton Club, where Hamp had played so many times. His casket was placed in a horse-drawn carriage, and as David Ostwald's Gully Low Jazz Band, accompanied by Wynton Marsalis, began the march to Riverside Church, people from around the world gathered to pay tribute.

William and Christian Dupin, a father and son from France, held up their cell phones so friends back home could hear the slow and powerful dirge. Emotions ran high, and in his intensity, the bass drummer went through his drumhead with his mallet.

It was a warm day, and the march took longer than expected. A man who worked at the church put his arm around me as we looked out at the assembly and said, "I know those old horses, and no one is going to hurry them."

I believe he was right. I could feel Hamp still working the crowd, as he was "Flying Home."

After a stirring poem read by the Rev. Dr. James Forbes, Jr., the tribute came to an end. The casket was returned to the horse-drawn carriage and carried back to the Cotton Club. It was then loaded into a hearse and taken to Woodlawn Cemetery in the Bronx.

As we passed his grave, many of us who loved and cared for Hamp placed a rose on his casket. I felt the sweetness that filled the air came not only from the flowers, but from the knowledge that Hamp was now with his God, the many friends who had preceded him, and his loving wife Gladys.

CHAPTER 34

A Visit to Russia

AS A RESULT OF THE FESTIVAL BRINGING IN SOVIET musicians beginning in 1989, Elvon and I were invited by the Russian Minister of Cultural Arts to participate in a jazz tour of Moscow and southwestern Russia in 1998.

We left Seattle on May 25 at 8:00 p.m. on Russia's international airline, Aeroflot, and we arrived in Moscow at 5:30 p.m. the following day. We were a little anxious about going through customs at the Moscow International Airport, but a young woman from Seattle who worked in Russia was very helpful, and we walked through without any trouble. We were met by Lembit Saarsalu, our saxophone-playing friend from Estonia, who was with us most of the time from that point on during our stay. We were very glad to see him and pleased to know he would be with us for twelve of our fourteen days in Russia.

After our luggage was loaded into a van, we went upstairs to have a drink of water or juice. It was to be our first warm drink of many to follow, as well as our first visit to a Russian restroom. Was it ever bad for the men! The women's restroom was not quite as bad, but it still was pretty horrible.

We rode from the airport to Red Square in an old Isuzu bus. I had never experienced anything like the feeling I had when we walked onto Red Square and I realized the importance of freedom to the Russian people. It was too late to take photographs, but the beauty of the square was something to behold. We saw the Kremlin Wall and many churches. Vendors on the square sold everything—books, photographs of former Soviet life, dolls, hats, and so on.

After a short visit to the square, we went to a small restaurant and had a salad and some borsch—a Russian soup made with beets and other vegetables. It was the first time I had tried it, and it had a flavor I was not accustomed to. After dinner we went to the train station and waited in a beautiful building for the train. It cost a few rubles just to wait there, and there were troops around to make sure everyone paid. The chandeliers and artwork in the station were marvelous. It was past one in the morning when we left the area, and the elevators were not in service. One of our new Russian friends said, "Everything in Russia stops at one in the morning."

On the night train to Kursk we were assigned to a sleeping car with Lembit Saarsalu and Evelyn White. The ride was quite rough, however, and the train's bathroom was terrible. Neither Elvon nor I could sleep. All night I thought of how my father had ridden in the caboose of the train when he took lambs to market from southern Idaho to Omaha, Nebraska, in the 1940s and '50s.

We arrived in Kursk at ten the following morning and were met by a crew of helpers to take us to our hotel. We met a marvelous man who had a car they called a Russian Cadillac. He drove us everywhere we wanted to go, including every rehearsal and concert. When we arrived at the hotel we were told there would be no hot water during our three-day stay. We would have to use water that was heated with an electric coil that looked like the device I used back home to start charcoal for the barbecue. Nonetheless, we managed to get ready for the first concert of the tour.

The concert included John Stowell and Evelyn White from the US, three French artists, and a group from Kiev, Ukraine, called ManSound, which was similar to the American group Take 6. ManSound later performed a few times at the Lionel Hampton Jazz Festival—the first time in 2000.

I played piano and Lembit played sax on "Oh Here's to You," a tune of mine dedicated to Lionel Hampton. I also did a piano solo on an original tune, "I Remember Yesterday." The entire group ended the concert doing an uptempo tune of mine called "Cajun Style Blues," the number we used to close each of the tour's ten concerts. The artists really seemed to get into it—as the composer, it was a kick for me to witness that. Russian jazz pianist Leonid Vintskevich played for most of the groups at the first concert.

I learned to say "I love you" in Russian, and the audience appreciated my attempt at that. They went wild as I told them through an interpreter how much the people in America loved them. My wife and I were invited to meet with several Russian dignitaries during intermission, and we were treated to the finest foods and beverages. We were both very tired from the trip and the eleven-hour time change. After the concert, which lasted more than five hours, we went to have something to eat with the other artists.

The next morning we were taken to a Catholic monastery, which had been mostly destroyed by the Communist government. The one building that remained after the 1991 change in government was being restored as a museum. Even the monastery's so-called holy water spring had been destroyed, but I was told that when it was destroyed, several other artesian springs were discovered in various parts of the country. The well at the monastery had been restored in 1991, and we were able to drink from it.

I played more of my tunes at the second concert, which was not quite as long as the first one. The music was very well received, and I was touched by the way the crowd reacted. We met with more Russia dignitaries during intermission. Someone had told them my wife and I didn't drink alcohol, so we had juice waiting for us at each of our meetings with mayors, governors, and other important politicians.

More than thirty musicians from Russia, the US, France, and Ukraine were involved with the third concert—another five-hour event that featured much new music from various parts of the world. It was obvious the audience was very up on jazz.

After three concerts in Kursk, we left by bus for the city of Orel, which was the Coca-Cola bottling capital for southwestern Russia. It was fun to see the excitement of the young and old alike when they received the many gifts that were donated to each concert by Coca-Cola. The company also provided an additional $75,000 to support the concert tour.

The trip to Orel took about four hours. After we had been on the bus for two hours, enjoying the beautiful forest along the road, the bus driver pulled over and one of the natives who also spoke English said, "Girls to the left, boys to the right!" At first I thought it was some kind of Russian humor, but as I saw one of the three women aboard the bus and more than thirty men get off and head for the forest, I knew those trees would be the only restroom we would see on this trip. Elvon and Evelyn were shocked, but on the next trip they found the strength and willpower to do what they needed to do.

The accommodations in Orel were quite nice. We even had hot water to take a shower and finally get ourselves really clean. The food was quite good, too. One of the foods we enjoyed was a special kind of bread that was just a little sweet. In fact, we thought all the breads were very good at that place. Elvon and I are not vegetarians, but we became known as such on the trip because we were concerned about the meat. The meat probably was just fine, but it didn't look as appetizing as the vegetables.

The Orel concert started at six in the evening, in an outdoor amphitheater. It was a large area, and there were several hundred people listening to the music. Never have so many people wanted my autograph on a poster or card. My arm and hand got tired from signing my name. Now I have an idea of how Hamp must have felt about signing autographs, even though he never said a word about it, but just thanked those who wanted his autograph.

This concert had an electric piano, and it ended up working quite well. I didn't get a chance to check it out ahead of time, but I took my chances and programmed it like I thought it should be, and it worked.

Lembit and I played "Oh Here's to You" and captured the audience with the way we played a ballad. Then I played "I Remember Yesterday," and by the way the audience responded to the piece, it was almost as if they knew my reason for writing it. We all have a tendency to remember yesterday. I actually wrote the piece in Skinner Canyon near Nounan, as I stared up at 10,000-foot Sherman Peak. I remember as boy looking up the canyon, which was named after my ancestors, trying to imagine what it was like to settle that valley.

I also had the pleasure of introducing Evelyn White each night. She sang very well and captivated the audience with her sound, which was much like Carmen McRae in her younger years. Evelyn accompanied herself on three tunes and the house trio backed her on some others.

The next morning we had a little time before we had to leave Orel, so we walked around for a while. The area around the hotel was beautiful, including a park dedicated to the war. We saw the remains of one of the city's oldest buildings, which had been destroyed in 1943. The pillars in front of this remaining structure were magnificent. After a short walk and a few photographs, it was time to get on the bus and head for Tula. We were able to buy some bottled Russian mountain spring water for the trip, and it was great. We also had some Pepsi Light, a small bag of peanuts, and one candy bar to share on the bus ride.

It was going to be somewhat of a longer trip to Tula, and I was concerned about the accommodations. I didn't know for sure what we might have as far as a bathroom, hot water, or whatever. This was one of those seven-hour bus rides, so I knew what this meant for two of the American women on the bus when the driver pulled over and the announcement was made: "Girls to the left, boys to the right!" I also knew what it meant to me. Growing up on a farm in southeastern Idaho, I knew I was okay if I could find a good tree for cover. It was tougher for the women, but they managed it.

I noticed much of the housing in Tula was very old and run-down. The little houses of the peasant farmers were practically in shambles, but they were still occupied. My fears about our stay in Tula were realized as we reached our hotel. Old hotels were not uncommon, but the room was pretty bad, and the restroom was very dirty. Later I learned I should have insisted on a better room.

The long bus ride and strange new foods had left my wife feeling a little ill, so she stayed up in the room for lunch before the concert. I was very hungry, however, so I went with the group to eat. We boarded the bus and half an hour later we stopped at a strange-looking place. We went around to the back door of the building and down a winding hall with cement walls. When we got to the place where we were to eat, I couldn't believe what I was saw. There were white linen cloths on the table, and the entire room was beautiful. I was told it had been a special meeting place for the Communist leaders when they came to Tula. I was concerned about my wife, however, and soon we were on our way back to the hotel.

When we got back to the hotel I found Elvon had been locked in the room, and there was no way to unlock the door from inside without a key. I was concerned because I could see that she had been very upset. This was not a good experience, and I told myself I would never again leave her for any reason.

Thousands of people came to hear the concert, which took place in a huge, beautiful park. The audience was very astute, and as with most of the places we had performed in Russia, most of the audience seemed to recognize the standard jazz tunes.

We left Tula very early the next morning for the seven-hour ride to Tambov. The concert was to be performed in a great concert hall that had been built by Stalin in the 1930s. When we arrived in Tambov, we saw the hotel was quite old. But it was right next to the concert hall, and we figured we could just walk to the concert. We were quite surprised when we walked into the hotel. It was clean, and the staff was helpful and friendly. Still, we went up to our room not knowing what to expect, and we were thoroughly surprised again. I have never seen a nicer suite of rooms in any hotel in the United States. Our room was completely new, with an incredibly clean and white bathroom, and every part of the room was exquisite. The restaurant made a special dish for us—a stew with potatoes, carrots, and mushrooms, along with some delicious bread and bottled water.

In Tambov we learned that jazz was one of the first outside music genres to come into the Soviet Union. Because most jazz doesn't have lyrics, it was less threatening to the Soviet leaders, who were trying to keep the citizens from being exposed to outside ideas.

As we walked around to the front of the hall, we were told its architectural style, with its impressive pillars, was definitely a Stalin-era design. Many of the Russians were offended that anyone would call the Stalin architecture beautiful. Later, we saw the inside of the building, with portraits of Russian composers on the walls. I had studied music history in college, and I recognized many of them.

The piano I played at the concert hall that night was a high-quality, well-tuned nine-foot grand piano made in Estonia. It was another great crowd, and afterward I signed a lot of autographs. We were very tired after the performance, so we skipped the usual post-concert meal, returned to the hotel, and went to bed early. The next morning we felt rested, and after a good breakfast, we were ready for our journey to the next town. We learned that Rachmaninoff had written many of his famous works in Tambov. We didn't have time to visit the site of his home, but we were touched by the history lesson we received. Rachmaninoff is one of my favorite composers.

As we left Tambov and the beauty of this marvelous city with its flowers and wonderful people, I asked if there was any way we could take our hotel room with us for the rest of the trip. Our Russian friend Leonid laughed. He may have laughed because he thought my line was pretty funny. More likely it was because he knew what was coming up. We were headed to Lipetsk, an industrial city of 700,000.

We were supposed to stay at a so-called resort, but when we arrived, we saw it was not good. The room was dirty, and there was not even a lid on the toilet. Our Russian friends could tell we were not pleased, and in less than an hour we were in the presidential suite of a new hotel, with the largest bathroom I've ever seen. It was luxury and cleanliness at its finest. Evelyn stayed with us in the suite, and had her own special part of the room, with her own bathroom and bedroom.

The concert at Lipetsk was held in a great hall, and it was a wonderful experience. Jazz was relatively new to that part of Russia, but we were treated with absolute kindness and respect. At the beginning of the concert we were asked to come onstage, and a girl, perhaps nine years old, came out and presented us with a beautiful loaf of bread with a small cup of salt in the middle. The bread was on a nice plate and the plate was on a long flowing piece of linen. After the ceremony, the interpreter told us that, according to tradition, this little girl, dressed in ancient dress, was supposed to give me the bread, and that I was supposed to take a piece of the bread, dip it in the salt, eat it, and give the little girl a kiss on the forehead. Of course, I didn't know about this until it was too late. But I'm sure the audience understood as I said "spasibo" (thank you) many times. It was a very touching ceremony.

Our professional interpreter and translator for the concert, a man named Serghej M. Shishkin, was an expert on Russian history, and he told us the story of Lipetsk. He said it had been a small town of about 10,000 people—mostly peasant farmers—when Stalin decided it would be a good place to bring people from other parts of the Soviet Union. Stalin was afraid people living in their own homes would be too comfortable with the conditions, and it might remind them of their former freedom. The city's population grew from 10,000 to 500,000, and workers were brought in to live in less-than-desirable living conditions. Some of those terrible conditions were still evident on our visit.

At this particular concert at Lipetsk, many of the artists were able to hear my tunes for the first time. Their response was very positive, and I could see their hearts were touched. I felt a special connection with these people. The director of the symphonic orchestra told me how much he enjoyed my compositions—that meant so much to me. We also heard a group of folk-jazz artists from Kursk who performed in original Russian folk costumes.

Then we were on our way to Voronezh. As we traveled along in our bus, we became quite hungry, so the driver stopped by a little place along the road. I thought it was someone's home or some kind of shop, but it actually was a roadside café. Inside it was very clean, and the food was wonderful. The people working at the café tried so hard to make our visit a memorable experience, and they succeeded. There was a river nearby that had the largest frogs I have ever seen in my life. They were five times larger than any frog I'd ever seen. The sound of the frogs was so powerful I felt as though I was in a frog concert.

When we arrived in Voronezh, the first person I met was Leonid Vintskevitch's close friend, Yuri Vermenich, who could be called the Leonard Feather of Russia. This man had single-handedly made a difference in jazz in Russia, even though the KGB was all over him, threatening his life for writing about jazz and for getting recordings for the artists. In fact, he was very close to Leonard Feather, and was familiar with the Lionel Hampton Jazz

Festival and the artists who had performed there over the years. I appreciated what Yuri had done for jazz in Russia. It is amazing to me how one person can make such a difference in a difficult society if he or she believes in a cause and is not willing to give up on the future.

The hotel room in Voronezh was nice and clean, and the impressive Stalin-era concert hall was within walking distance. The concert went very well, and again I played on a very good nine-foot grand piano. The audience was really into jazz and loved every tune they recognized. They really knew the jazz standards. Again, there was much autograph signing. I gave a signed Lionel Hampton Jazz Festival poster to Yuri.

As we prepared to leave Voronezh we saw several buildings that were typical Stalin-Soviet architecture. But there were thousands of people in the city buying food, clothing, and various things at a little marketplace. It was amazing to see the capitalistic changes. At least goods were available. It had not been long before when there were very few goods to be purchased unless one had plenty of money or was connected to a high-ranking member of the Communist government.

I remember so well the three times that we had artists from the former Soviet Union at the Lionel Hampton Jazz Festival—in 1989, 1990, and 1991. Even in 1991, when eighteen musicians came, the woman in charge (I thought she was a KGB agent) told the Soviet artists that we had rigged one store to have all of the things on the shelves as propaganda for the United States. However, by the time she left Moscow, Idaho, even she had been convinced that things were much different in a free society. We took her to several different stores and she couldn't believe the general public had access to so many things.

It was time to leave Voronezh and go to Belgorod, our last concert in this region of Russia. When we arrived in Belgorod, after having traveled some of the only four-lane roads in the country, we were taken to a hotel to eat and dress for the concert.

We had no time for a sound check or to determine the quality of the piano. The hotel was in pretty bad shape and very dirty. However, there was a most beautiful view of the city from our room. The grounds around the hotel were also very beautiful. Belgorod is also called "the white city" because of the minerals that are mined there. The city itself was very beautiful.

We were told that many of the city leaders did not want a jazz concert in Belgorod, but I found those in attendance to be most appreciative of the music, and many seemed to enjoy my songs. It was a feast or famine place for sure. The piano turned out to be not very good. It took so much strength to play, but so little sound came out. After the concert, we had a delicious lunch and then headed to the station to board the train for the twelve-hour ride to Moscow.

When we got to the station we had to walk across the tracks and up some strange platforms to wait for the train. It was a little nicer than the train we had ridden from Moscow to Kursk several days earlier, but I was dreading the all-night ride. It turned out okay, though, because we were so tired that we actually slept for the first full night. This was the first time in Russia that I had room to straighten my legs at night. The restrooms on the train were not very good, but were still better than those on the first ride. We had good bottled spring water to drink.

At the train station in Moscow we were met by our original bus and taken to the Rossiya Hotel. The first room they showed us was not acceptable, but a few minutes later we were taken to a very nice room for our three-day stay in Moscow.

We were to perform in the famous Tchaikovsky Hall, and it was a great privilege. We had to shorten the show, however, because we were allowed only three-and-a-half hours. But it all worked out well. I had read about this great hall, but I never imagined I would perform there. I had another well-tuned nine-foot Estonian grand piano, and Lembit and I again had a great time. We learned that the original owner of the hall, a wealthy Jewish man, was not trusted by Stalin and was taken from the building one night. He was brought to a Siberian labor camp, and the hall came under the ownership of the government. But at the time of our visit, the building was no longer owned by the government.

The next morning we had a few hours to spend with Lembit, and he showed us Red Square. He took us to Moscow's oldest church, which had been converted to a museum. We also visited Lenin's tomb. Cameras were not allowed in the mausoleum, so Lembit waited outside with the cameras and the rest of us went inside. There was Lenin, encased in glass as if he had been there just a few hours. There was not a blemish on his skin. We were later told that Russia has a very fine embalming school and a special way of doing this art.

We then went to a mall on the square that had goods from Russia, Europe, and the US—basically anything you could want. That was a long way from the late 1980s and early 1990s, when even Russian items were scarce. I decided I wanted one of those Russian fur hats that are worn in the winter, and was told those were the kind worn by party leaders in the Soviet era. We then went to a beautiful park on Red Square that was very close to the gates of the Kremlin. A tractor that looked like it was from the 1940s was being used to pick up trash.

It was soon time for Lembit to go on with his part of the tour with Evelyn White, Leonid Vintskevich, and John Stowell. They were going down to Penza for three days of concerts, and then to St. Petersburg.

Then we spent two days with a marvelous guide named Cyril Moshkow, who was a journalist and editor for Russia's only jazz magazine. He had been born and raised in Moscow and spoke English, so we learned firsthand from someone who really knew the city and its history. We saw the oldest parts of the city, the KGB headquarters, the headquarters for the Communist leaders, and a store where only Communist leaders could shop. We took a boat ride on the Moscow River and saw a park built on the site of Stalin's former home, which was now a special place for foreign presidents and dignitaries to stay while visiting Moscow.

Cyril told us most Soviet leaders did not want Soviet musicians to play jazz because it represented the US and the West. The government tried to persuade the people that everything from Europe or America was bad and that the people could do without it.

We had Saturday afternoon and one more day in Moscow, and then we would fly back to the US. On Saturday afternoon we went on a tour with Cyril. I bought the fur hat I had wanted, and a few matryoshka dolls, and then we went on a seven-hour walk through the city. We could not have managed it with without Cyril, who gave us lessons in Russian history, culture, and art along the way. We saw the old KGB building where all of the records of the people were kept. Lembit told us he was able to see the 128 pages of records that the KGB had kept on him. He said, "Here I am—a jazz musician who never gave anyone a problem at any time, and I had 128 pages. I wonder how many pages were kept on the people with problems."

We saw the headquarters for the Communist government, and the housing area where many of the Communist leaders lived. We saw many buildings that were taken over in 1917 by the Soviet government after the owners were sent to Siberia. We went to a McDonald's to use the restroom and were told the hamburgers at the Moscow McDonald's were much tastier than those at an American McDonald's. We had already eaten, so we didn't get the chance to find out for ourselves.

It was amazing to see these old buildings and to learn about their history. We also had the opportunity to see the remains of the original wall that had surrounded Moscow in the twelfth century. The wall was thick and well built, and we felt as if we had been taken back in time several hundred years.

When we finally arrived back at our hotel we were extremely tired but excited to have seen all of the marvelous sights. After a little rest, we went to one of the little restaurants in the hotel for something to eat. The view from the hotel at that time of night was exquisite.

Cyril was busy on Sunday morning, but he met us in the hotel that afternoon for our last day of touring. He asked us if we would like to go inside the Kremlin walls—something I was not aware was allowed. As we prepared to enter, we were told all purses and backpacks had to be left with security. We were a little concerned, but we took a claim check, and when we returned, our things were exactly as we had left them.

Inside the Kremlin, we were awed by the beautiful buildings, including many churches that were being restored. We saw cannons that were used against Napoleon in 1812, and the world's largest cannon, which had never been fired. The ball for the cannon was about three feet high, and it was a sight to behold.

We were then taken to see the remnants of a bell that became dislocated from the top of one of the churches during the Napoleonic Wars, when the entire city of Moscow was burned. Originally, the bell was as big as a house, and after it fell, one of the broken pieces was still about fifteen feet high. We were told the bell had made the lowest possible sound that could be heard by the human ear. All the bells in the church towers we saw were magnificent. We were told they were only rung when there was a special message for the people.

We then went into a brand-new shopping mall that was as nice as any in the US. It was three stories, and had restrooms that cost two rubles to use. We rode the subway built by Stalin in the 1930s. The subway station was decorated with marble and beautiful chandeliers, and the ceilings and walls were covered in art. The subway train traveled about sixty miles an hour, so you got where you were going quickly. After our subway ride, we took a boat ride the entire length of the city on the Moscow River. The boat ride was a beautiful experience that allowed us to see the city from a new perspective.

Moscow University, which was mostly built during the Stalin era, and completed three years after his death, is near the park that was built on the grounds of his former home. Despite numerous "No Swimming" signs, hundreds of students were blatantly ignoring the warning. As I looked into the polluted river, I decided I wouldn't want any part of my body in it.

We saw the world's largest sports pavilion, which seats 250,000, and new hotels, including many US chains. After the fantastic boat trip and our new knowledge of the old and new Moscow, we were wishing we had several more days to explore the majestic city. But it was time to pack our few gifts for our children and grandchildren and get ready to fly to Seattle the next morning.

We slept very little, but morning soon came, and Cyril was waiting to go with us in our taxi to the airport, so we wouldn't be nervous about getting to our plane. He knew exactly where to take us and what to do.

We had a few moments before boarding our plane, so we went shopping at the duty-free shop. We were told the ceilings of the airport had been covered with thousands of painted coffee cans at the beginnings of the new government in 1991. Then we were on Aeroflot again, on our way to Seattle. In real time, we arrived a little more than ten hours later—but with the time zone changes, we arrived in Seattle thirty minutes before we left Russia!

We were so glad to be in Seattle and so close to Moscow, Idaho, which was now just an hour away by plane. The first thing we bought in the Seattle airport was a banana, because we were so hungry for fruit. When we got back to Idaho, our humble home looked like a mansion compared to what we had seen in Russia. Thanks to our friends in Russia and the Russian Minister of Cultural Arts, we had experienced so much in just two short weeks. More than anything, we learned how fortunate we were to live in the US.

From Abate to Zeitlin

Below is a list of artists who performed at the Lionel Hampton Jazz Festival during my years as director. My apologies to anyone who may have been inadvertently missed.

Greg Abate, Charles Abeles, Alex Acuña, Ashley Alexander, Monty Alexander, Brenda Alford, Geri Allen, Eric Allison, John Allmark, John Allred, Helio Alves, Ernestine Anderson, Ernie Andrews, Reiko Aoki, Ron Aprea, Stephen Armour, Jay Ashby;

Claudio "Tony" Barrero, Kenny Barron, Clare Bathé, Brian Blade, Terence Blanchard, Andrés Boiarsky, Patti Bown, Curtis Boyd, Gerald Brazel, Randy Brecker, Adam Brenner, Matt Brewer, Ron L. Bright, Mike Brignola, Bud Brisbois, Brian Bromberg, Ray Brown, Matthew Brubeck, Lance Bryant, Dan Buckvich, Herman

Burney, Dwayne Bumo, Jon Burr, Kenny Burrell, Gary Burton, Igor Butman, Gerald Byrd;

Obed Calvaire, Conte Candoli, Pete Candoli, Gerald Cannon, Lisa Capers, Dave Carpenter, Terri Lyne Carrington, Arnie Carruthers, Betty Carter, Regina Carter, Michael Carvin, Marc Cary, Bill Charlap, Doc Cheatham, Renato Chicco, Buddy Childers, Billy Childs, John Clayton, Don Coffman, Anat Cohen, Joe Cohn, Lionel "Freddy" Cole, Richie Cole, Jeff Colella, Ira Coleman, Billy Contreras, Carla Cook, Keith Copeland, Eve Cornelious, Anthony Cox, Albert "Chip" Crawford, Ronnie Cuber;

Duduka da Fonseca, Sasha Daltonn, Clare Daly, Dee Daniels, Jim Day, Santi Debriano, Buddy DeFranco, Angela DeNiro, Cynthia Dewberry, Eldar Djangirov, Doctor Blues, Leon Dorsey, Paquito D'Rivera, Ray Drummond, Gary Duchaine, Bobby Durham;

Harry "Sweets" Edison, Peter Eldridge, Ken Elliott, Herb Ellis, Ethel Ennis, Billy Erskine, Rob Eschete, Robin Eubanks, Bill Evans, Andy Ezrin;

Christian Fabian (Bausch), John Faddis, Art Farmer, Leonard Feather, David Finck, Chuck Findley, Ella Fitzgerald, Tommy Flanagan, George Fludas, Kim Foley, Carl Fontana, Jimmy Ford, Frank Foster, Gary Foster, Caprice Fox, Ray Franks, David Friesen, Matsuko Fuji, Curtis Fuller, Larry Fuller;

Roberta Gambarini, Alan Gemberling, Gary Gemberling, Stan Getz, Terry Gibbs, Dizzy Gillespie, Joe Giorgiano, Lincoln Goines, David Goloshchokin, Benny Golson, Terri Gonzales, Richie Goods, Aaron Graves, Benny Green, Al Grey, Mike Grey, Brian Grice, James Griffen, Mike Guerrier, Eric Gunnison, Cleave Guyton;

Lionelle Hamanaka, Jeff Hamilton, Lionel Hampton, Locksley "Slide" Hampton, Roy Hargrove, Winard Harper, Gene Harris, Antonio Hart, Marion Hayden-Banfield, Jimmy Heath, Jon Hendricks, Conrad Herwig, Patience Higgins, Milt Hinton, Dave Holland, Shirley Horn, Steve Houghton, David Howe, Freddie Hubbard, Luther Hughes, William "Billy" Hulting, Paul Humphrey, Greg Hutchinson, Phyllis Hyman;

Sherman Irby, Illinois Jacquet, Al Jarreau, Jane Jarvis, Brent Jensen, Ingrid Jensen, Alex Jeun, Howard Johnson, William Johnson, Elvin Jones, Hank Jones, Harold Jones, Oliver Jones, Salena Jones, Willie Jones III;

Michael Karetnikov, Geoff Keezer, Primo Kim, Nancy King, Lauren Kinhan, Andrei Kitaev, Oscar Klein, Joe Kloess, Diana Krall;

Randy Landau, Don Lanphere, Andy Laverne, Dana Leong, Eric Lewis, Victor Lewis, Abbey Lincoln, Joe Lovano, Mundell Lowe, Carmen Lundy;

Gabriel Machado, Donvonte McCoy, Mark McGowan, Kevin Mahogany, Russell Malone, Junior Mance, Herbie Mann, Billy Marcus, Kitty Margolis, Sherrie Maricle, Branford Marsalis, Delfeayo Marsalis, Wynton Marsalis, Anibal Martinez, Feodir Marun, Ron Mathews, Kazu Matsui, Rich Matteson, Eric Matthews, Llew Matthews, Christian McBride, Barney "Mayor" McClure, Rob McConnell, Ron McCroby, Robert McCurdy, Roy McCurdy, Marshall McDonald, Ian McDougall, Bobby McFerrin, Gayelynn McKinney, Marian McPartland, Carmen McRae, Darmon Meader, Gary Meek, John Michalak, Kuni Mikami, Volodymyr Mikhnovetsky, Mulgrew Miller, Pete Minger, Jane Monheit, James Moody, Dado Moroni, Jiro "George" Mraz, Gerry Mulligan, Rob Mullins, Romano Mussolini;

Lewis Nash, Kim Nazarian, Amy Nelson, Jeff Nelson, Steve Nelson, David "Fathead" Newman;

Anita O'Day, Herb Ohta, Karen Oleson, Eileen Orr, Alexandre Ouzounoff;

Aaron Parks, Matt Parrish, Nicki Parrott, John Pendenza, Ralph Penland, Danilo Pérez, Bill Perkins, Sam Pilafian, Bucky Pizzarelli, John Pizzarelli, Valery Ponomarev, John Poole, Benny Powell, Zack Pride, Tito Puente;

Kenneth Rampton, Lou Rawls, Joshua Redman, Della Reese, Dianne Reeves, Barry Ries, Pat Rickman, Karriem Riggins, Ben Riley, George Robert, Curtis Robinson, Justin Robinson, Claudio

Roditi, Mickey Roker, Yuri Romensky, Wallace Roney, Billy Ross, Jorge Rossy, Jim Rotondi, Jimmy Rowles, Vanessa Rubin;

Lembit Saarsalu, , David Sánchez, Arturo Sandoval, Stephen Scott, Chris Severin, Doc Severinsen, Grant Seward, Bud Shank, Marlena Shaw, George Shearing, Bobby Shew, Arkady Shilkloper, David Schumacher, Ricardo Silveira, Edward Simon, Michael Slivka, Lew Soloff, Ed Soph, Jan Stentz, Charles Stephens, Grant Stewart, Shirley Stewart-Farmer, Curtis Stigers, John Stowell, Karolina Strassmayer, E.J. Strickland, Vladimir Sukhin, Neil Swanson;

Buddy Tate, Grady Tate, Joel Taylor, Clark Terry, Toots Thielemans, Ed Thigpen, Ruben Tolmachov, Brian Torff, David Torkanowsky, June Townes, Vladimir Trach, Robert Trowers, Bobby Tucker, Stanley Turrentine;

Jeff Uusitalo, Eric Vaughn, Sarah Vaughan, Frank Vignola, Leonid Vintskevich, Nick Vintskevich;

Walt Wagner, Myron Wahls, David T. Walker, Walter Wallace, Cedar Walton, Kenny Washington, Peter Washington, Bill Watrous, Wally Gator Watson, Jeff Watts, Jerry Weldon, Frank Wess, Jiggs Whigham, Rodney Whitaker, Evelyn White, Ben Wittman, David Widelock, Sunny Wilkinson, Bruce Williams, David "Happy" Williams, Joe Williams, John B. Williams, Steve Williams, Larry Willis, Lisa Wilson, Nancy Wilson, Ben Wolfe, Anthony Wonsey, Jimmy Woode, Phil Woods, Gail Wynters, Chihiro Yamanaka, Greg Yasinitsky, David Young, Andy Zadrozny, Denny Zeitlin.

CPSIA information can be obtained
at www.ICGtesting.com
Printed in the USA
LVHW071545190719
624654LV00015B/218/P

9 781629 015873